WRITING
Computer Code
Code

by Chris Minnick
Eva Holland

WILEY

WRITING COMPUTER CODE

Published by
John Wiley & Sons, Inc.
111 River Street
Hoboken, NJ 07030-5774
www.wiley.com

For general information on our other products and services or to obtain technical support, please contact our Customer Care Department within the U.S. at 800-762-2974, outside the U.S. at 317-572-3993, or fax 317-572-4002.

Wiley also publishes its books in a variety of electronic formats. Some content that appears in print may not be available in electronic books.

Library of Congress Control Number: 2016941390

ISBN 978-1-119-17730-2 (pbk); ISBN 978-1-119-17732-6 (ebk); ISBN 978-1-119-17733-3 (ebk)

Manufactured in the United States of America

10 9 8 7 6 5 4 3 2 1

CONTENTS

INTRODUCTION

SO, YOU WANT TO GET STARTED WRITING REAL COMPUTER CODE! Maybe you've played with drag-and-drop programming languages or you've done modding in Minecraft, and you're ready for the next level. Great! There are currently more than 500 different languages for coding on computers (which isn't very many, when you consider that there are about 6,500 human languages!). You're about to learn the most popular languages that are used by millions of coders all over the world.

ABOUT THIS BOOK

In this book, you'll learn to use HTML5, CSS3, and JavaScript to create programs for computers. More people have used these three computer-coding languages than any other coding language that's ever been invented. In fact, every single website that you visit makes use of these three languages. That's why we think you've made a great decision by beginning your journey into the world of coding by picking up *Writing Computer Code*.

Computer code is fun and easy to learn. With some determination and a lot of imagination, you'll be creating your very own computer programs in no time!

Just as the only way to become a great athlete or musician is to practice, practice, practice, the only way to become a computer programmer is to write code, write code, write code!

This book is put together as a series of projects with steps for constructing each project from start to finish. The projects also build upon one another, so that by the end of the book you'll have an animated robot that you can control with your mouse and continue to modify and improve long after you finish all the projects.

Here's what you need to do the projects in this book:

» A computer running the Windows, Mac OS X, or Linux operating system

» A web browser, like Chrome, Firefox, or Safari

» An Internet connection

As you work through each project, keep in mind the following:

» Code and web addresses are in monofont. If you're reading this as an ebook, you can click web addresses, like www.dummies.com, to visit that website.

» When you're getting started, the best way to learn is to see how other people do it. For this reason, we've included pictures for every important step in the book, and all our examples are online at http://jsfiddle.net/user/watzthis/fiddles. If you want to check your work, or just copy ours, be sure to look at both of these.

» Every project wraps up with a last look at the project's big ideas in coding. The big ideas consist of codes and concepts you'll find useful for future projects.

» Coding isn't that hard, but it does come with a lot of technical details. If you don't feel like reading all the explanations, just skip ahead to the next code example and try it out.

ABOUT YOU

We already know that you're ready and willing to code. Because you're reading this, we know you're fully qualified and able to get started right away. We don't make many assumptions, but here are the things we wanted to mention upfront:

» **You should be comfortable with using a web browser to visit websites, and with typing on a keyboard.** The projects in this book won't likely work on a phone or tablet without a keyboard.

» **You're comfortable with very basic math.** We're talking about addition, subtraction, multiplication, and division. We don't require anything very advanced at all, but basic math is an important part of programming.

» **You have the patience and dedication to stick with it and troubleshoot bugs.** We guarantee that programming can be a lot of fun, but we also guarantee that it can be frustrating when you have to track down the one typo or missed command that is making your whole program not work. Stick with it!

That's really all there is to it. If you get stuck, keep in mind that many problems in writing computer code happen simply because of spelling errors or words that you type that a computer can't understand. Proceed slowly and carefully, and you'll do great!

ABOUT THE ICONS

As you read through the projects in this book, you'll see a few icons. The icons point out different things:

Watch out! The Warning icon marks important information that you can use to avoid common pitfalls when coding.

The Remember icon marks concepts you've encountered before and should keep in mind while coding.

The Tip icon marks advice and shortcuts that will help you create code and graphics quickly and easily.

The Fun with Code icon describes how the coding you're doing relates to the bigger picture of computer programming.

The Fun with Math icon describes the everyday math you use while coding computer programs. Finally, you see how that stuff really is used!

THE FIRST STEP

Once you take your first steps down the road of writing code, the world of computers will open up to you and you'll be able to use your computer to do some pretty amazing things. You'll also join the community of millions of programmers around the world as we shape the web and the future! Congratulations on taking the first step!

PROJECT 1 BECOMING A PROGRAMMER

COMPUTERS CAN'T DO THINGS ON THEIR OWN. They need a computer program to tell them what to do, and they need people to write those computer programs. The people who write the code to make computers do all sort of things are called *computer programmers.*

WHAT IS PROGRAMMING?

A *computer program* is a group of instructions that can be understood and followed by a computer. Another name for a computer program is *software. Computer programming,* also known as *coding,* is what we call it when we write these instructions.

Figure 1-1 shows a computer program.

Right now, this computer code may look confusing, but after you've read this book, you'll understand how to read it and even write it yourself!

```
1   <div id="robot">                                    HTML ⚙
2   <div id="head">
3       <div class="eye" id="righteye"></div>
4       <div class="eye" id="lefteye"></div>
5       <div id="nose"></div>
6       <div id="mouth"></div>
7   </div>
8   <div class="arm" id="rightarm"></div>
9   <div id="body"><p id="message">I Love to Code!</p></div>
10  var rightEye = document.getElementById("righteye");  JAVASCRIPT ⚙
11  var leftEye = document.getElementById("lefteye");
12  var leftArm = document.getElementById("leftarm");
13
14  rightEye.addEventListener("click", moveUpDown);
15  leftEye.addEventListener("click", moveUpDown);
16  leftArm.addEventListener("click", moveRightLeft);
17
18  function moveUpDown(e) {
19    var robotPart = e.target;
20    var top = 0;
21
22    var id = setInterval(frame, 10) // draw every 10ms
23
24    function frame() {
25      robotPart.style.top = top + '%';
26      top++;
27      if (top === 20){
28        clearInterval(id);
29      }
30    }
```

```
1   body {                                               CSS ⚙
2       font-family: "Comic Sans MS",
3   cursive, sans-serif;
4   }
5   p {
6       font-size: 3em;
7   }
8   .eye {
9       background-color:blue;
10      width:30%;
11      height:30%;
12      border-radius: 50%;
13  }
14  .arm {
15      background-color: #cacaca;
16      position: absolute;
17      top: 35%;
18      width: 5%;
19      height: 40%;
20  }
21  #head {
22      width:30%;
23      height:30%;
24      border-radius: 15%;
25      background-color: #dadada;
26      position: absolute;
27      left: 32%;
28      top: 5%;
29  }
30  #righteye {
```

Figure 1-1: The computer program you'll make in this book!

The computers of today are much more powerful than ever before. It used to take a whole room of computers to do what we can now do with even the smallest computer. One thing all computers have in common, no matter how powerful, is that they need computer programs to do anything and they need computer programmers to write these programs.

Computer programs help people to do many things, including the following:

» Playing music and videos

» Performing scientific experiments

» Designing cars

» Inventing machines

» Playing games

» Controlling robots

» Guiding satellites and spaceships

» Creating magazines

» Teaching people new things

THE WOMEN WHO INVENTED PROGRAMMING

Electronic computers were first invented in the 1930s. But it was in the middle of the 1800s when the first computer program — a set of instructions designed to be carried out by a machine — was written.

The author of the first computer program — and the world's first computer programmer — was a woman named Ada Lovelace. She was a mathematician who lived in England. Ada imagined that computers would be able to do all the things we use computers for today, including working with words, displaying pictures, and playing music. Her unique understanding earned her the nickname "The Enchantress of Numbers." We're guessing your nickname isn't as rad as that.

The computer that Ada Lovelace wrote programs for didn't look anything like the computers of today. Instead of a plug or battery, it had a crank! Check out this photograph of Charles Babbage's Difference Engine, one of the very first computers.

(continued)

(continued)

Photograph courtesy of Jitze Couperus
(https://commons.wikimedia.org/wiki/File:Babbage_Difference_Engine_(Being_utilised).jpg)

In order for computer programs to be converted into machine language, we need to use compilers. *Compilers* are programs used to convert programming languages into machine language. The very first compiler was created by Grace Murray Hopper in 1944. Her invention led to computer programs being able to run on different types of computers, and eventually gave birth to JavaScript. Grace Hopper is also the inventor of the term *debugging*, for fixing problems in computer programs. This term was inspired by the removal of an actual moth from an early computer. Grace Hopper became known as "The Queen of Software" or "Amazing Grace" for her contributions to modern computing. (What can we say? Nicknames were just cooler back then.)

The computers that Grace Hopper worked on used electricity (not cranks), and they were huge, as you can see in this photograph, which shows the Colossus computer. Colossus was the first programmable electronic computer.

Photograph courtesy of Bletchley Park Trust/Science & Society Picture Library (www.flickr.com/photos/101251639@N02/9669449367)

Can you think of other things that computers can do?

All computer programs begin with an idea. Before you start writing any code, it's important to think about what you want your program to do. Use your imagination and dream big!

Here are some helpful questions to think about before you begin coding:

» What will my program do?

» Who will use my program?

» Why will they use my program?

» Where will they use my program?

» How will they use my program?

HOW CAN YOU TALK TO COMPUTERS?

Every computer program is written using a computer programming language. Programming languages allow you to write instructions that can be translated (or compiled) into machine language. These programming languages are eventually turned into *binary codes,* which use zeros and ones to form letters, numbers, and symbols that can be put together to perform tasks.

At the heart of every computer is a central processing unit (CPU), shown in Figure 1-2.

The CPU is made up of millions of tiny, very fast switches (called *transistors*) that can be on or off. The position of these switches determines what the computer will do. Software, written by programmers, tells these switches when to turn on or off by using binary codes.

Every single thing that a computer does is the result of a different combination of many zeros and ones. For example, to represent a lowercase letter *a*, computers use the following binary code:

```
0110 0001
```

Source: https://commons.wikimedia.org/wiki/File:Cpu.jpg

Figure 1-2: At the heart of every computer is a CPU.

Each zero or one in a binary number is called a *bit,* and a combination of eight bits is called a *byte.* When you hear the words *kilobyte, megabyte,* and *gigabyte* used to tell how big a file is, what that means is the number of bytes it takes to store the file.

Table 1-1 lists the most common storage sizes.

TABLE 1-1   HOW MANY BYTES IS THAT?

Name	Number of Bytes	What It Can Store
Kilobyte (KB)	1,024	Two to three paragraphs of text
Megabyte (MB)	1,048,576	800 pages of a book
Gigabyte	1,079,741,824	1,000 books
Terabyte	1,099,511,627,776	1 million books
Petabyte (PB)	1,125,899,906,842,624	Several copies of every book ever written!

WRITING NUMBERS IN BINARY CODE

Do you want to learn to count like a computer? We'll show you how to write any number between 0 and 255 in binary code. For this example, we'll write the number 150 in binary code.

1 Write the following numbers horizontally at the top of a piece of paper:

128	64	32	16	8	4	2	1

These numbers are your binary cheat sheet.

2 Underneath these numbers, write the number that you want to convert to binary, which is 150.

3 Start with the first number you wrote on your paper, 128. If this number fits inside of 150, write a 1 under it. If it doesn't fit inside of 150, write a 0 under it.

Because 128 *can* fit inside of 150, put a 1 under the 128.

128	64	32	16	8	4	2	1
1							

4 Subtract the number 128 from the number you're writing in binary code (150): 150 – 128 = 22. Cross out the 150 that you wrote down and write down 22.

5 Compare the remainder to the next number in your binary cheat sheet, 64. Does 64 fit inside of 22? It doesn't, so write a 0 under 64 and move on to the next number in the cheat sheet, 32.

6 Because 32 doesn't fit inside of 22, write a 0 under the 32, and move on to the next number, which is 16.

7 Ah ha! 16 does fit inside 22! Write a 1 under the 32 and then subtract 16 from 22: 22 – 16 = 6. Cross out the 22 and write down 6.

8 Take a look at the next number. Does 8 fit inside of 6? It doesn't, so write down a 0 and move on to the next number.

Continue doing these steps until you reach the last number of the binary cheat sheet. In the end, you should have the following:

128	64	32	16	8	4	2	1
1	0	0	1	0	1	1	0

Now you know that 10010110 is the binary code for 150.

A typical small computer program might contain anywhere from a couple kilobytes to a couple megabytes of instructions, images, and other data. You don't have enough time in your busy day to type out thousands of ones and zeros. Because computers can't understand what you mean when you speak your language, if you want to tell a computer what to do, you need to learn to write in languages that computers can understand.

WHAT LANGUAGES WILL YOU LEARN?

People have created hundreds of different computer languages. In this book, we focus on the three languages that make the World Wide Web work: HTML, CSS, and JavaScript. Together, these three languages can be used for so many different things, including building apps for an iPhone; making super cool, interactive websites; and even designing videogames that you can play on your computer!

In the early days of the Internet, web pages only included plain text. Some of the text varied in size, and sometimes there were links between different web pages. This was made possible by a computer language called HTML.

HTML stands for Hypertext Markup Language, which is a fancy way of saying that HTML can be used to turn text into links, but it can also do much more, as you'll soon see.

In those early days, there weren't different fonts or pretty layouts. We barely had any pictures, and there certainly wasn't any animation! Figure 1-3 is an example of one of the first web pages.

We aren't complaining, though. When the web was new, it was really exciting to click from one page to another and discover new things. Even more exciting was how easy it was for anyone to publish things and have anyone else on the Internet be able to read it!

Pictures, colors, forms, and many other features were introduced very quickly after this. CSS was invented to make web pages look prettier (see Figure 1-4)!

CSS stands for Cascading Style Sheets. It adds styles — like colors, borders, and backgrounds — to HTML code.

Figure 1-3: An example of one of the first web pages.

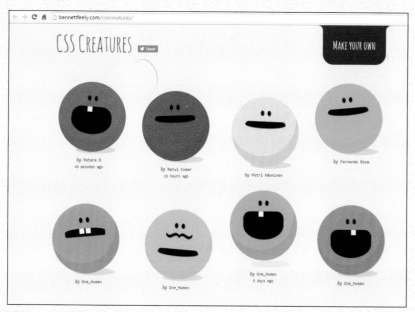

Figure 1-4: CSS Creatures lets you make your own creature using CSS!

Soon, people wanted ways to be able to play games, create animation, and make web pages that would respond to commands and clicks. In other words, people wanted interactivity!

To make web pages interactive, JavaScript was created. Whenever you visit a website and see something moving, or you see things appearing and changing on the page, chances are, it's JavaScript at work.

To see some great examples of websites that combine HTML, CSS, and JavaScript to do amazing things, open up your web browser and visit the following sites:

» **Nature Valley Trail View (http://naturevalleytrailview.com; see Figure 1-5):** Nature Valley Trail View has more than 300 miles of National Parks trails captured and preserved using a combination of HTML, CSS, and JavaScript.

Figure 1-5: Exploring the trail!

» **Draw a Stickman (www.drawastickman.com; see Figure 1-6):** Draw a Stickman is a super fun website where you can draw your own character and creatively interact with different episodes, all powered by JavaScript and HTML!

Figure 1-6: Your custom stickman can go on adventures!

» **The Interactive Ear (www.amplifon.co.uk/interactive-ear; see Figure 1-7):** The interactive ear lets you learn and explore how ears work. Best of all, this site was built using the languages you'll learn in this book!

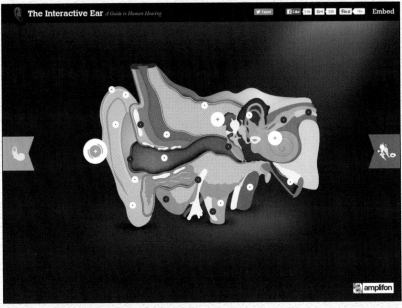

Figure 1-7: The human ear is so interesting!

GATHERING YOUR TOOLS

Every task you complete requires a set of tools, and writing
computer code requires some special tools as well. Instead of
things like hammers and pencils, JavaScript programmers use
tools that are found on the Internet. You'll only need a web
browser and an Internet connection to complete all the projects
in this book.

Let's move on and get your toolbox organized.

GETTING YOUR BROWSER READY

The one essential tool that you need for working with JavaScript
is a web browser. You have many different web browsers to
choose from, and nearly all of them will do a great job running
JavaScript. You probably already have a web browser on your
computer.

The most widely used web browsers today are Mozilla Firefox, Apple Safari, Google Chrome, and Microsoft Internet Explorer. For this book, we'll be using Chrome, which is currently the most popular web browser and has a number of great tools for working with JavaScript.

If you don't already have Chrome installed, you'll need to download and install it. You can install Chrome by opening any other web browser and going to www.google.com/chrome/ browser/desktop. Follow the instructions found on that page (shown in Figure 1-8) to install Chrome on your computer. When you have Chrome installed, start it up.

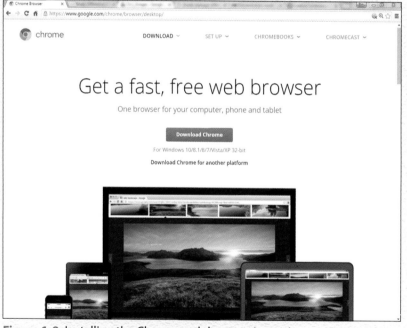

Figure 1-8: Installing the Chrome web browser is easy!

WORKING WITH JSFIDDLE

We'd like to introduce you to our favorite JavaScript playground: JSFiddle. Instead of swings and slides, you'll be playing with JavaScript statements, HTML tags, and CSS styles.

JSFiddle lets you write and experiment with code from within your web browser. You can use it to try out code, get feedback on your code, share your code, and even work on programs with your friends!

JSFiddle is what we'll be using throughout this book to experiment with HTML, CSS, and JavaScript. It's called JSFiddle because you can use it to "fiddle" with code. So, let the fiddling begin!

To get started with JSFiddle, open your Chrome web browser and type http://jsfiddle.net into the address bar. You'll see a screen that looks like Figure 1-9.

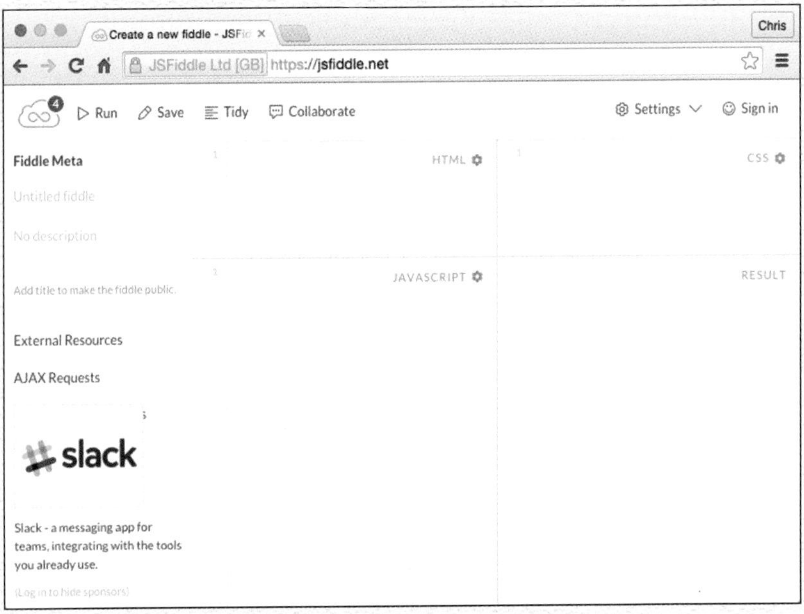

Figure 1-9: The JSFiddle home page, your new playground.

JSFiddle is made up of three panes where you can enter each of the three types of web code: HTML, CSS, and JavaScript. The fourth pane is the Result pane, where you can see the results of what you type inside the other boxes. The toolbar on the left lets you add a title and description to your project and has some other advanced features we won't worry about for this book. The top toolbar has buttons for running, saving, and cleaning up your code.

CREATING A JSFIDDLE ACCOUNT

JSFiddle lets anyone create an account and share their programs in a public dashboard — and many excellent and very experienced programmers do!

When programmers share their programs on JSFiddle, they agree that anyone who wants to can make a copy of their work, change it, and republish it. However, it's always polite to give the original author credit when you borrow code.

Creating a JSFiddle account isn't required in order to proceed with the book, but it will make viewing and sharing your work easier.

Follow these steps to create a JSFiddle account:

1 Click the Login/Sign Up link in the upper-right corner of the screen.

2 Click the Sign Up link under the login form.

3 Fill out the Create an Account form and click Create an Account.

The Edit Your Profile page appears.

4 If you would like, you can make changes here and save them.

5 When you're ready to start fiddling, click the Editor link at the top of the screen.

You can resize any of the panes in JSFiddle by clicking and dragging the border that separates them.

For now, we're going to focus on the JavaScript pane. Follow these steps to run your first JSFiddle program:

1 **Click inside the JavaScript pane.**

2 **Type the following JavaScript statement:**

```
alert("Hi, everyone!");
```

3 **Click the Run button on the top toolbar. A pop-up window containing the message "Hi, everyone!" appears.**

4 **Click OK to close the pop-up window.**

Congratulations! You just wrote your first JavaScript program! Running JavaScript isn't the only great thing JSFiddle can do. With JSFiddle, you can also use the HTML and CSS panes to run code that works together with your JavaScript code. You'll see each of these panes in more detail in the next few sections. But first, let's take a quick look at what JSFiddle is capable of doing!

The CSS pane in JSFiddle is located in the upper-right corner. CSS allows you to change how stuff such as text and graphics look. If you want to change the color of the text on your page, you use CSS.

Follow these steps to try out changes to one of our programs:

1 **Go to http://jsfiddle.net/watzthis/oboLdy4p.**

Make sure to type this address carefully, including the capital letters in the right spots. If the animation doesn't work for you, check that the address starts with http:// *and not* https:// *and fix that.*

2 **Take a closer look at each of the four main areas of the screen: Three of them have some code in them, and the Result pane is displaying floating bubbles animation.**

Can you figure what any of this code might do?

3 **Look at the CSS pane in the upper right: You see three lines of code.**

You may need to click and drag on the border of the CSS pane to make it bigger so that you can see everything in it.

4 **Find the code that reads** `border: 3px solid yellow;` **and change it to** `border: 8px solid black;`.

Make sure *not* to type a period at the end of what you're typing. The period ends our sentence, but it doesn't end the code you're typing.

5 **Click the Run button in the top toolbar to start the animation over.**

The bubbles are now much thicker (as shown in Figure 1-10)!

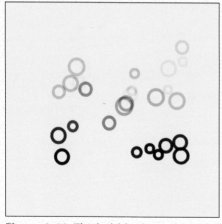

Figure 1-10: The bubbles have thick walls!

Based on the change that you just made and the effect that it had, what do you think the part of the code that says `solid` does? To find out, try the following steps:

1 **In the CSS pane, change the first value after `border:` to a smaller number (such as 2 or 3) and click Run.**

The circles get thin again!

2 **Change the word `solid` after `border:` to one of the following words:**

   » Dotted

   » Dashed

   » Double

   » Groove

   » Ridge

   » Inset

   » Outset

3 **Click Run to see what it does.**

This tells what style the border of the bubbles should be!

Now take a look at the third value after `border:`, which is currently set to `black`. This controls the color of the bubbles.

Follow these steps to change the color of the bubbles:

1 **Pick your favorite color, such as blue or red or green.**

2 **Replace the color name `black` in the CSS pane with your new color name.**

3 **Click Run.**

Your bubbles are now your favorite color!

Now take a look at the HTML pane, in the upper-left corner. Compared to the CSS and JavaScript panes, this one doesn't have very much in it!

HTML is used to create structure for web pages and containers for JavaScript programs to run in. In the case of this Bubbles program, the HTML just creates the place on the page for the bubbles to go into.

But you can do much more with HTML! To make some changes to the HTML for the Bubbles demo, try the following:

1 **Put your cursor after `</div>` and type the following:**

```
<h1>I love bubbles!</h1>
```

Your HTML pane should now have the following HTML code:

```
<div id="o"></div>
<h1>I love bubbles!</h1>
```

HTML code works by adding special codes around regular text. Adding codes to text in this way is called marking up text.

2 **Click Run to see your changes in the Result pane (see Figure 1-11).**

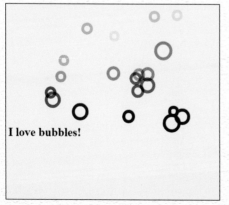

Figure 1-11: The bubbles now have a special message below them!

In HTML, `<h1>` and `</h1>` are known as *tags*. Tags around text tell the browser that the text represents something special. In this case, `<h1>` represents a first-level header, the largest and most important header on the page.

Another very useful HTML tag is the `<p>` tag, which marks paragraphs. To insert a `<p>` tag, follow these steps:

1 **After the `</h1>` tag, press Return (Mac) or Enter (Windows) to move to the next line.**

2 **Type `<p>` and then type any message that you want to display.**

JSFiddle automatically creates your closing `</p>` tag.

3 **Click Run to see your message appear in the Result pane.**

The JavaScript pane, in the lower-left part of JSFiddle, is where really interesting things happen.

1 **In the JavaScript pane, find the line that reads `max = 36` and change it to `max = 80`.**

2 **Click Run.**

Many of the bubbles, but not all of them, are now larger than they were before.

Based on the behavior of the bubbles when you changed the value of `max`, can you guess what will happen if you change the line that reads `min = 12`? Try it out and see if your guess is correct! If you guessed that `max` controls the maximum size of the bubbles and `min` controls the minimum size of the bubbles, you're absolutely right.

The next two lines in the JavaScript pane are `bubbles = 100` and `timerDelay = 8000`.

Try changing both of these values and see what happens. By playing around with these values (or maybe just by guessing), you'll discover that `bubbles = 100` tells how many bubbles there should be, and `timerDelay` has something to do with how fast the bubbles rise.

SHARING YOUR FIDDLE

Now that you've created your own personalized version of the Bubbles demo, it's time to show your friends!

1 Click the Share button in the top toolbar.

You'll see the options to copy the address for your Bubbles demo, to view the program in full-screen mode, and to share your program on Facebook or Twitter.

If you want to share your programs on Facebook or Twitter, remember to tag us (@watzthisco on Twitter or www.facebook.com/watzthisco), and we'll check out your creations!

2 Highlight the full-screen URL in the Share menu, as shown in Figure 1-12, and copy it by pressing ⌘+C (Mac) or Ctrl+C (Windows) or by choosing Edit ⇨ Copy in your browser.

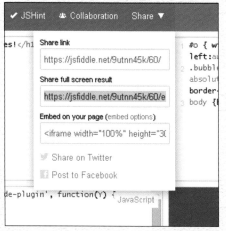

Figure 1-12: Highlighting the full-screen URL.

3 Open a new browser window tab (by pressing ⌘+T [Mac] or Ctrl+T [Windows]) and paste the full-screen address into the address bar.

The bubbles display onscreen without the code panes.

If the Bubbles demo doesn't work for you in full-screen mode, try changing the https *in the browser address bar to* http *and press Return or Enter.*

If you want to return to the original Bubbles program, you can do so by going back to our public dashboard at https://jsfiddle.net/user/forkids/fiddles.

SUMMARY

In this chapter, you learned what computer programmers do and experimented with writing some code in JSFiddle. In the next chapter, we explore the language of JavaScript and show you the special rules of writing in JavaScript.

PROJECT 2 GATHERING THE PARTS TO BUILD YOUR ROBOT

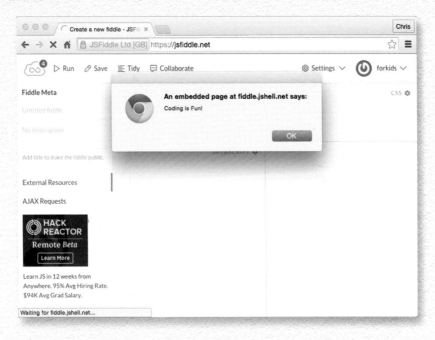

JUST AS SPOKEN LANGUAGES HAVE RULES (CALLED GRAMMAR), COMPUTER PROGRAMMING LANGUAGES HAVE RULES (CALLED SYNTAX). When you understand the basic rules of speaking JavaScript, it actually looks similar to English.

If you think that your teacher correcting you when you say "ain't" is strict, wait until you see how strict JavaScript is! It won't even listen to a thing you say if you make certain kinds of syntax errors.

When you write in a human language, your sentences are made up of different parts, such as nouns and verbs (see Figure 2-1).

In JavaScript, sentences are called *statements*. Statements are made up of different parts, such as *operands* (which are like nouns) and *operators* (which are like verbs).

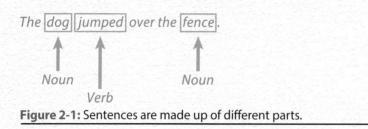

Figure 2-1: Sentences are made up of different parts.

In this chapter, you learn the basics of JavaScript syntax, and discover how operands and operators work in JavaScript programs.

SAYING WHAT YOU MEAN

As a programmer, your job is to think about what you want your program to do, and then to break it down into small steps that the computer can do without making any mistakes. If you wanted to ask a robot to go downstairs and make you a sandwich, you might start your instructions like this:

1 **Rotate head toward stairs.**

2 **Use visual sensors to look for obstacles.**

3 **If an obstacle is found, figure out what it is.**

4 **If the obstacle is a cat, try to lure the cat away from the top of the stairs by**

» Throwing a toy down the hall

» Speaking the cat's name

» Gently nudging the cat with your hand until it walks away

5 **If there is no obstacle, rotate left foot in the direction of the stairs.**

6 **Place left foot in front of right foot.**

7 Look for an obstacle.

8 Determine whether you're at the top of the stairs.

9 If you're not at the top of the stairs, rotate right foot in the direction of the stairs.

10 Place right foot in front of left foot.

11 Repeat steps 1 through 10 until you're at the top of the stairs.

You've already written 11 instructions and the robot hasn't even begun to walk down the stairs! A real computer program to tell a robot to go downstairs and make a sandwich would need much more complicated instructions than the ones shown here. At each step along the way, each motor would need to be told exactly how long to turn on, and each possible obstacle would need to be described in detail.

All these instructions would need to be written as individual JavaScript commands, or statements.

MAKING A STATEMENT

In English, we talk in sentences. In computer code, a single instruction to the computer is called a *statement*. Like a sentence, statements are made up of different parts and have rules that they must follow in order to be understood. A computer program can be made up of many statements, or even of just one statement.

The following statement causes a web browser to open up a popup alert with the sentence "Coding is Fun!"

```
alert("Coding is Fun!");
```

If you type this statement into the JavaScript pane in JSFiddle and press Run, you'll see something like Figure 2-2.

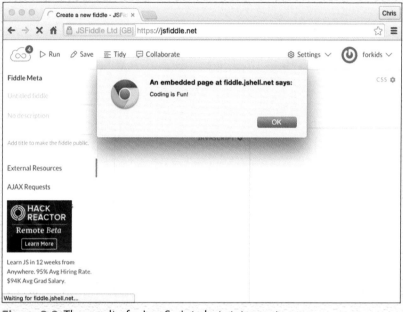

Figure 2-2: The result of a JavaScript alert statement.

Notice that the statement contains a keyword (`alert`), some symbols (parentheses and quotes), and some text (`Coding is Fun!`), and ends with a semicolon (`;`).

Just as an infinite number of sentences can be written using English, an infinite number of statements can be written with JavaScript.

The word `alert` is an example of a JavaScript keyword. Many JavaScript statements begin with keywords, but not all of them do.

The semicolon is what separates one statement from another, just as a period separates one sentence from another. Every statement should end with a semicolon.

FOLLOWING THE RULES

JavaScript has several rules that must be obeyed if you want your computer to understand you. Here are the most important rules:

» Spelling counts.

» Capitalization counts.

» Spacing doesn't count.

Coding languages are *very* picky about spelling. They're so picky, in fact, that they don't even like it when you capitalize something wrong, for example, by typing **Alert** instead of **alert**.

When a programming language cares about capitalization, we call it case sensitivity. *This name comes from the fact that it's so sensitive about whether you use uppercase or lowercase letters.*

The only time when this strictness doesn't apply is when text is surrounded by double quotes (") or single quotes ('). When that happens, spelling errors won't cause problems. You can type whatever you want!

In our "Coding is Fun!" example, you can replace the words inside the double quotes with anything you want! For example, you can add your name like this: "My name is Eva, and I think coding is fun!"

If you type anything outside of the quotes, you have to follow the rules; otherwise, your program may not run at all.

GIVING AND RECEIVING DATA

Programs come in many different sizes and have many different purposes. Here are three things all computer programs have in common:

» All computer programs have a way to receive information from a user.

» All computer programs have a way to give information back to a user.

» All computer programs have a way to store and work with the information.

Information, or data, that a program receives from a user is called *input*. What the program gives back to a user is called *output* (see Figure 2-3).

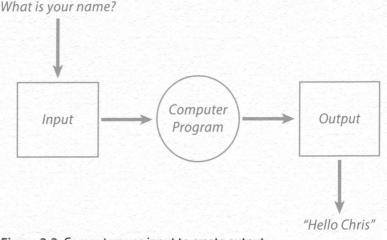

Figure 2-3: Computers use input to create output.

In the real world, when you want to store something, give something away (as a gift, for example), move something, or organize something, you often put it in a box.

Computers don't care about heart-shaped boxes of chocolates or shoeboxes with the latest sneakers inside them. What computers love is data. And to store and move around data, computers use a special kind of box called a *variable.* A variable is a box you can assign a name to. This name will represent all the information contained in that box, or variable.

Variables make it possible for one program to work with a variety of different input and produce different output.

Follow these steps to create and use variables:

1 **Click the JSFiddle icon in the upper-left corner of JSFiddle to open a new fiddle.**

2 **Type the following into the JavaScript pane to create a variable called** myBook**.**

```
var myBook = "Writing Computer Code";
```

3 **Click Run.**

If you did everything correctly, nothing will seem to have happened.

4 **Type the following on the next line in the JavaScript pane:**

```
alert(myBook);
```

5 **Click Run.**

A popup window will appear containing the words Writing Computer Code (see Figure 2-4).

As you can see, creating a variable in JavaScript is pretty simple! To create a variable, you use the var keyword, followed by the name of the variable, like this:

```
var myBook
```

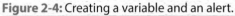

```
≡ Tidy    💬 Collaborate          An embedded page at fiddle.jshell.net says:          ×

                                  Writing Computer Code

                                                                        OK


    var myBook = "Writing Computer Code";                        JAVASCRIPT ⚙
    alert(myBook);
```

Figure 2-4: Creating a variable and an alert.

Notice how we separate words in variable names by using capital letters for every word after the first one. Variable names can't contain spaces, so programmers have created several other ways to separate words. This particular style is called camelCase. Can you guess why it has that name?

As a programmer, you have a lot of freedom in naming your variables. You can get very creative when you name your variables, but you don't want to get too crazy. Most important, your variable names should describe what you store inside of them.

The following variables have good and descriptive names:

```
var myFirstName
var favoriteFood
var birthday
var timeOfDay
```

Just by looking at these variable names, you can probably guess what kind of information is stored inside them.

After looking at these examples, what would you name variables for storing the following information?

» Your pet's name

» Your favorite school subject

» The name of your best friend

» Your street address

Here's what we might call these variables:

» myPetName

» myFavoriteSchoolSubject

» bestFriendName

» myStreetAddress

In addition to the rule that variable names must not contain spaces, there are several other rules that you must follow:

» Variable names must begin with a letter, an underscore (_), or a dollar sign ($).

» Variable names can contain only letters, numbers, underscores, or dollar signs.

» Variable names are case sensitive (capitalization matters!).

» Certain words may not be used as variable names, because they have other meanings within JavaScript. These so-called reserved words are as follows:

break	case	class	catch
const	continue	debugger	default
delete	do	else	export
extends	finally	for	function
if	import	in	instanceof
let	new	return	super
switch	this	throw	try
typeof	var	void	while
with	yield		

When creating your variables, you only need to type **var** when you first create and name them. When you want to use or change what's inside your variable, you only need to use that variable's name.

When you have stored data in a variable, you can recall it at any time during your program by typing the variable name. So, when you use the variable name `myFavoriteFood` inside your program, it's exactly the same as saying "tacos."

Let's try it out!

1 After the last statement you typed in the JavaScript pane, type the following:

```
myBook = "JavaScript For Kids";
```

2 On the next line, type this:

```
alert(myBook);
```

3 Click Run.

The first popup will appear, just as before with the title `Writing Computer Code`.

4 Close the first popup window by clicking OK.

A second popup will appear, containing the title JavaScript For Kids (see Figure 2-5).

Notice that the same alert statement was used to pop up two different book titles. This is just one of the many amazing things that are possible using variables.

The data inside a variable can also be called the value of a variable.

```
 e   ≣ Tidy    ⬚ Collaborate        An embedded page at fiddle.jshell.net says:        ×

                                     JavaScript For Kids

                                        Prevent this page from creating additional dialogs.


                                                                          OK




   1  var myBook="Writing Computer Code";                        JAVASCRIPT ⚙
   2  alert (myBook);
   3  myBook = "JavaScript For Kids";
   4  alert(myBook);
```

Figure 2-5: Opening a second popup with a different book title.

KNOWING YOUR OPERANDS AND OPERATORS

In JavaScript, when a piece of code causes something to happen, such as adding two numbers together to get another number, we call this piece of code an *expression*. For example:

$$1 + 1 = 2$$

Expressions are made up of operands (like the number 1) and operators (such as = or +).

Operands can be words or numbers or even variables.

When a variable contains a value, it can be used anywhere that you would normally use that value.

An *operator* is a symbol that performs a task (or an operation) using the operands.

Figure 2-6 shows the different parts of a JavaScript statement.

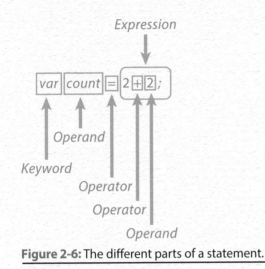

Figure 2-6: The different parts of a statement.

JavaScript has many different operators that handle many different needs. Instead of showing you a list of all the operators, we wrote a program that lets *you* choose operators and operands and then see the results!

Meet the Super-Calculator! It can work with words and letters, as well as numbers.

INTRODUCING THE SUPER-CALCULATOR

You've never seen a calculator like this before. This calculator can do addition, subtraction, multiplication, and even division!

That's not all! This Super-Calculator can take words and stick them together! Let's say you have the word *Java* and you have the word *Script,* and you want to somehow glue them together. Impossible, you say? Not with the Super-Calculator!

How does this amazing Super-Calculator work? How can you get one? We're about to tell you, and your world will never be the same again!

FORKING THE SUPER-CALCULATOR

We've created this lovely calculator in JSFiddle. Simply follow these steps to open and create your very own version of it:

1 **Open your web browser and log in at** http://jsfiddle.net.

2 **Go to our public dashboard at** http://jsfiddle.net/user/watzthis/fiddles **and locate the program called Chapter 2 – Super-Calculator.**

The Super-Calculator fiddle opens (see Figure 2-7).

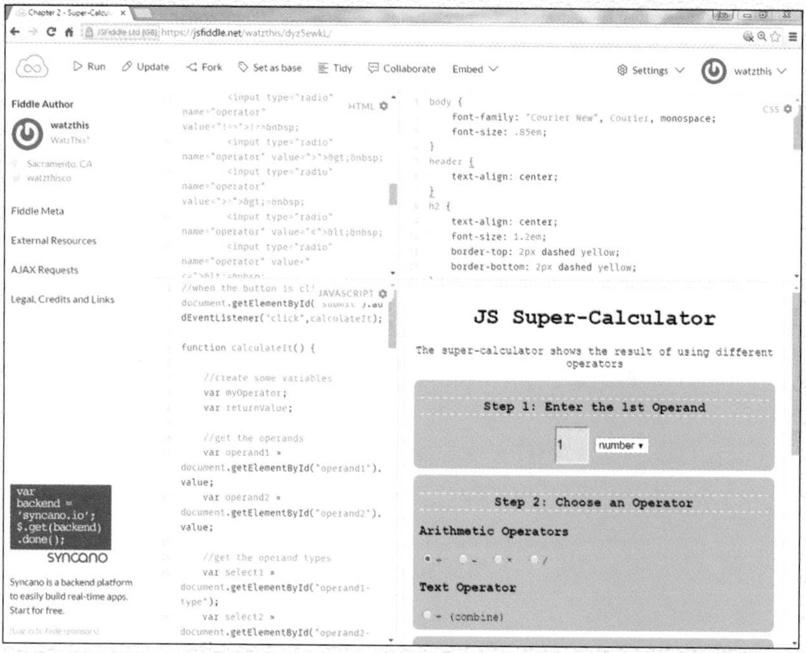

Figure 2-7: The JS Super-Calculator.

3 **Click the Fork button in the top menu to make a copy of the Super-Calculator in your own JSFiddle account.**

4 **Use the Fiddle Options in the left menu to change the name of your Super-Calculator to** *Your Name*'s **Super-Calculator.**

5 **Click Update in the top menu, and then click Set as Base.**

Now you have your own version of the Super-Calculator! You're ready to start learning how it works and using it to learn about operands and operators.

USING THE SUPER-CALCULATOR

The Super-Calculator allows you to see the result of using different operators. It features two places where you can put in operands, each with a drop-down menu where you can select the type of data you entered (number or text), and radio buttons for selecting an operator to use.

Radio button *is the name that HTML uses to refer to the circular buttons that can be grouped together. They're different from check boxes because you can only select one button in a group of radio buttons, but you can select multiple boxes in a group of check boxes. We think they're called radio buttons because they work in the same way as car radio station selection buttons. Pressing one button sets the station to that choice and deselects the others.*

To get started with the Super-Calculator, take a look at the settings that are in the Result window when you first open it.

You may want to resize the windows in JSFiddle to make your Result pane as large as possible.

The input area at the top, shown in Figure 2-8, contains a single value, the number 1. The input type drop-down menu is set to Number.

Under the input area for the first operand is where you select an operator. The operators are divided into two groups: arithmetic operators and text operators. Notice that the first operator in the group of arithmetic operators, +, is selected, as shown in Figure 2-9. This is the addition operator.

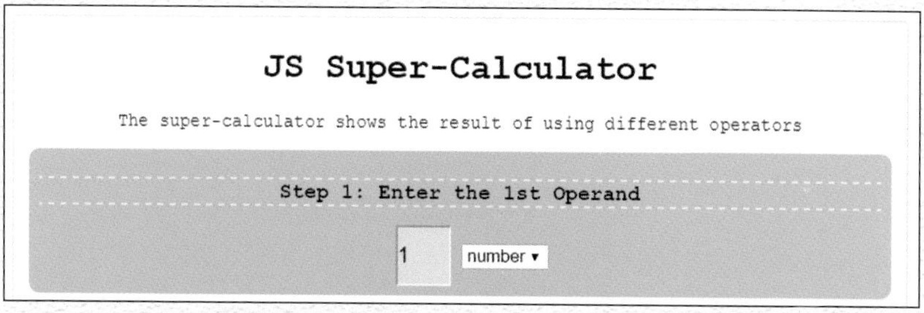

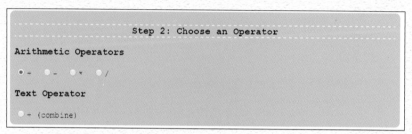

JS Super-Calculator

The super-calculator shows the result of using different operators

Step 1: Enter the 1st Operand

1   number ▾

Figure 2-8: The default value of the first operand is the number 1.

Step 2: Choose an Operator

Arithmetic Operators

● - ● _ ● × ● /

Text Operator

● + (combine)

Figure 2-9: The addition operator is selected by default.

Underneath the operator choice area is the input area for the
second operand. By default, this is set to the number 1 as well
(see Figure 2-10).

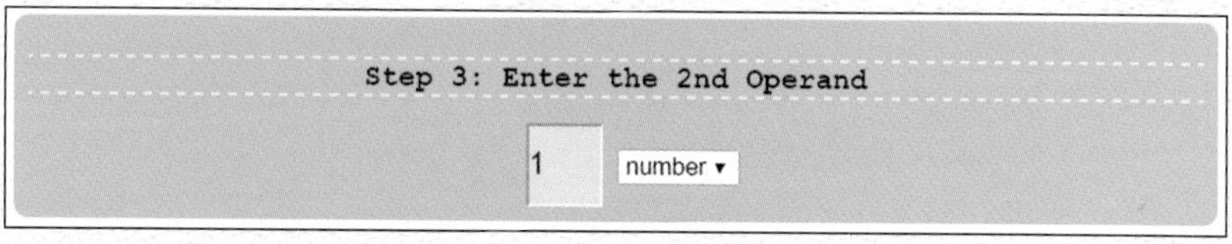

Step 3: Enter the 2nd Operand

1   number ▾

Figure 2-10: The second operand is set to the number 1.

When we put this all together, the default operation for the
Super-Calculator is the world's most basic math problem: 1 + 1.

Click the Operate button at the bottom of the calculator. The
result displays at the bottom of the Output area (see Figure 2-11).

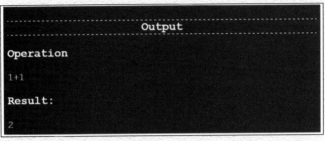

Figure 2-11: Adding numbers with the Super-Calculator.

Of course, you already knew the answer to that operation! Right now you may be thinking that this Super-Calculator isn't so super after all. Not so fast! Let's try a more difficult problem.

1 **For the first operand, enter the number 435.**

2 **For the operator, select the multiplication operator, *.**

3 **For the second operand, enter the number 888.**

4 **Click Operate.**

The result, 386280, comes back instantly, as shown in Figure 2-12.

Now, that's pretty super, right?

This is all just normal calculating that any calculator can do. Our Super-Calculator is unlike any calculator you've used before because it can also work with words! Move on to the next section to see how.

SUPER-CALCULATING WITH TEXT

Now let's try some operations that, while still simple (because they only involve two operands), will show you some interesting things about JavaScript.

1 **Leave the values of the operands set to their default (1 and 1), but select the text operator, + (combine), and change the data types for each operand to Text.**

Now, when you click Operate, you see that the result is 11 (see Figure 2-13).

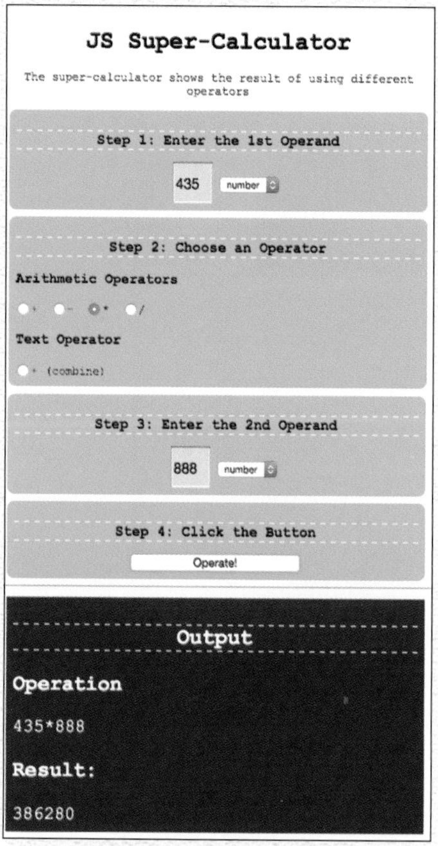

Figure 2-12: Multiplying with the Super-Calculator.

2 Leave the operator set to the Text operator, and leave the data types set to Text. Change the first operand value to Java and the second operand to Script.

3 Click Operate.

The result of combining Java and Script is shown in Figure 2-14.

4 Leave the operator set to the Text operator and both data types set to Text. Change the first operand to your first name, followed by a space, and change the second operand to your last name.

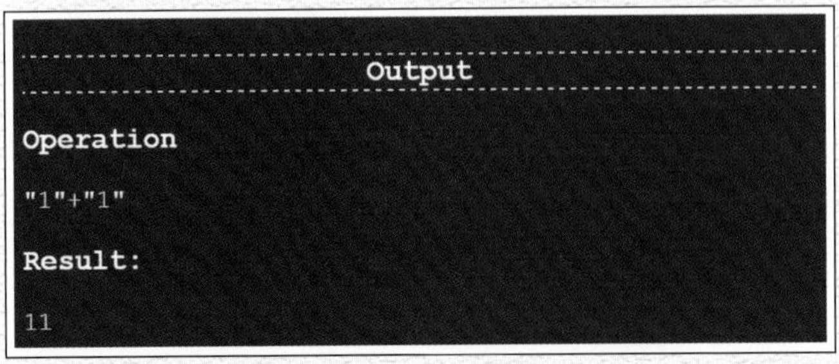

```
......................................................
                        Output
......................................................
Operation
"1"+"1"
Result:
11
```

Figure 2-13: The result of concatenating 1 and 1.

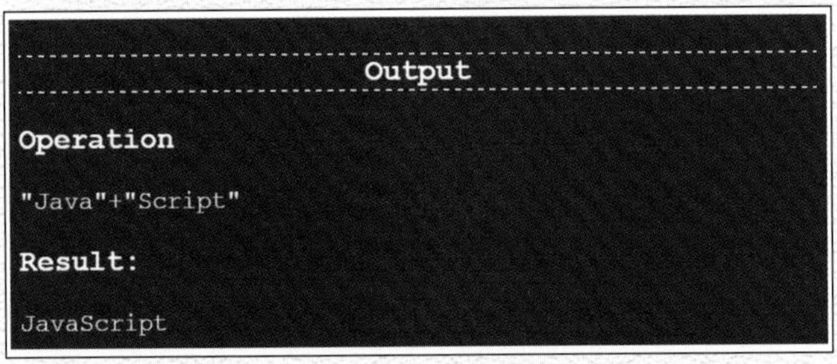

```
......................................................
                        Output
......................................................
Operation
"Java"+"Script"
Result:
JavaScript
```

Figure 2-14: Combining Java and Script.

5 Click Operate.

The result will be your first and last name, with a space between them. The important thing to learn from this example is that when you write in JavaScript, it will include any spaces you put in your operands.

6 Change the operator from the Text operator to any of the arithmetic operators. Leave both data types set to Text.

7 Click Operate.

The result, shown in Figure 2-15, is NaN, which means "not a number." There's no way for JavaScript to perform arithmetic operations using letters, and NaN is its way of telling you that.

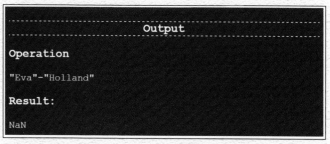

Figure 2-15: Trying to do math with your name results in NaN.

SUMMARY

In this chapter, you learned some important things about programming. You learned that variables are boxes that you can put values into. You also learned that programming "sentences" are called *statements*. Finally, you learned how to use operators and operands to form statements that can transform inputs into outputs. In the next chapter, we start building a robot that you'll be able to customize and animate using HTML, CSS, and JavaScript.

PROJECT 3 BUILDING YOUR ROBOT'S BODY

JAVASCRIPT, HTML, AND CSS GO TOGETHER LIKE CHEESE, PEPPERONI, AND PIZZA: YOU COULD HAVE ONE WITHOUT THE OTHERS, BUT WHY?

To get the most out of this mixture of JavaScript, HTML, and CSS, you need to know a little bit about how to use HTML to create a structure for your program.

In this chapter, we explore HTML and show you how to use JavaScript to work with HTML to build a robot.

WRITING HTML

HTML stands for *HyperText Markup Language*. That's a fancy way of saying that HTML is a language that you can use to create links (hypertext). HTML is so much more than simply a language for creating links, though.

HTML forms the skeleton that the text, pictures, and JavaScript in a web page attach to.

SEEING WHAT TEXT LOOKS LIKE WITHOUT HTML

Markup languages, like HTML, were invented in order to give documents (such as letters, books, or essays) structure that a computer can understand and do things with.

Here's a simple list that a person can understand with no problem:

```
Things I Need
carrots
celery
spinach
```

As a human, you see this list and understand it. But to a computer, this list has some issues. Figure 3-1 is what it looks like when you view the preceding list with a web browser.

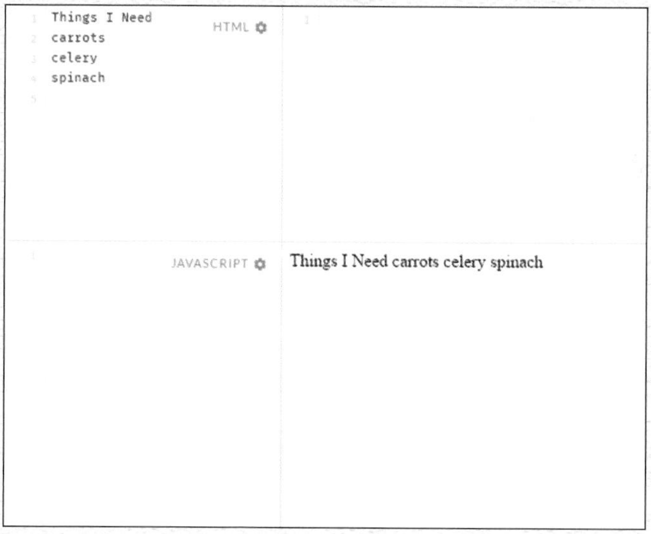

Figure 3-1: The list displayed as HTML in JSFiddle.

As you can see, a computer has no way of knowing that "Things I Need" is a title, or that the rest of the items are part of a list. To make this list understandable to a web browser, we need to use HTML to "mark it up."

USING HTML: IT'S ALL ABOUT THE TAGS

HTML is made up of tags. The tags on clothes give you information about what the clothes are made of and how to wash them. Similarly, tags in HTML give you information about the content inside of them.

Tags are made up of keywords inside of angle brackets (< and >) and they come in two basic types: a beginning tag and an ending tag. Here's an example of a beginning tag:

```
<p>
```

The p tag is how you mark up text in a document as a paragraph.

Most beginning tags also have matching ending tags. The only difference between a beginning tag and an ending tag is that an ending tag has a / before the name of the tag. For example, here's the ending p tag:

```
</p>
```

To use tags, just put the thing that you want to mark up (such as text, images, or even other tags) between the beginning and ending tags. For example, here's how you would mark up a paragraph of text in HTML:

```
<p>This is a paragraph of text. A paragraph has a
   line break before and after it in order to
   separate it from the other paragraphs of text in
   a document.</p>
```

HTML has a bunch of tags that you can use to label different parts of a document. Examples of tags include <p> for paragraph, <img> for image, <audio> for audio clips, <video> for video clips, <header> for the top of a web page, and <footer> for the bottom of a web page.

When you have a beginning tag, an ending tag, and stuff in between those tags, we call the whole thing an HTML *element*. Here are some more examples of HTML elements. You can try

each of these out to see what they look like by typing them into
the HTML pane in JSFiddle.

```
<p>An HTML <em>element</em> is made up of
    <strong>text</strong> and <strong>other
    elements</strong>.</p>

<h1>This text will display large and bold.</h1>

<h2>This text will be bold and smaller than h1
    text.</h2>

<h3>This text will be smaller than h2 text.</h3>

<header>Content in a header element is for the top
    of an HTML document or web page.</header>

<footer>Content in a footer element is for the
    bottom of an HTML document or web page.</footer>

<a href="link.html">This is a link</a>

<div><p>The div element creates a box where you can
    put anything you want, like
    paragraphs.</p></div>
```

Here's the list from earlier in the chapter marked up as an HTML
document, made up of tags and text:

```
<html>
  <head>
    <title>My Grocery List</title>
  </head>
  <body>
    <h1>Things I Need</h1>
      <ol>
        <li>carrots</li>
        <li>celery</li>
        <li>spinach</li>
      </ol>
  </body>
</html>
```

Figure 3-2 shows what it looks like when you view it with a web browser. That's much better, right?

Figure 3-2: The list displayed as HTML in a web browser.

Notice that you can't see the HTML tags in the web browser. Instead, they tell the web browser how to show text and images.

NESTING HTML TAGS

Writing HTML is pretty easy once you know a few things about how tags are put together. The first thing to know is that most HTML documents share a very similar basic structure, and they all must follow a few basic rules.

The first rule of writing HTML is that tags need to be opened and closed in the right order. One way to remember this is FILO, which stands for *First In, Last Out*.

Notice that the grocery list earlier starts with the `<html>` tag and ends with the `</html>` tag. This is how every HTML document should start and end. All the other tags in a web page are "inside" the `html` tags, and they're closed according to FILO.

For example, the `<head>` element is inside of `<html>`. Therefore, the closing `head` tag must come before the closing `html` tag:

```
<html>
    <head>
    </head>
</html>
```

The `<ol>` tag comes after the `<body>` tag, so `<ol>` is inside of `<body>` and you have to put the `</ol>` tag before the `</body>` tag:

```
<html>
    <head>
    </head>
    <body>
        <ol>
        </ol>
    </body>
</html>
```

HTML elements are put together in a similar way to Russian nesting dolls (see Figure 3-3). One element goes inside of another. Another word for the way HTML tags fit inside of each other is nesting.

Figure 3-3: HTML tags nest in the same way that Russian nesting dolls do.

Another rule when writing HTML is that documents always have a head element and a body element:

» **The** head **element:** The head element is like the brain of your web page. JavaScript code often goes into the head element, but it doesn't display in the web browser window.

   In the grocery list, we have only a title tag in the head. The title is what displays at the top of the browser window or in your browser's tab when you're on a web page. Whatever you put inside the title tag is usually what shows up as a link in search results, too.

» **The** body **element:** The body element is where everything that you want to display in the web browser goes. In the grocery list, we have several elements in the body:

   » **The** h1 **element:** The h1 element can be used to identify the most important header on your web pages. Headers typically identify sections of documents or web pages. For example, if this chapter were a web page, the first h1 element would come right after the chapter introduction and would read "Writing HTML."

   » **The** ol **element:** Following the h1 element, we have an ol element. ol stands for *ordered list*. An ordered list is a list of items that are numbered or lettered in a particular order. HTML also lets you make unordered lists, by using the ul (for *unordered list*) tag. Unordered list will display with a dot, or bullet, to the left of each item.

   » **The** li **element:** Following the ol element, we have an li element. Inside of either an ol or ul element, you can use any number of li elements (li stands for *list item*) to create the individual list items in your list.

WRITING YOUR FIRST HTML DOCUMENT

Now that you've seen the basic rules of HTML, you're ready to build your first HTML document.

1 **Open your web browser and go to** https://jsfiddle.net**.**

2 **Drag the pane borders to make the HTML pane in JSFiddle as large as you like.**

We're only going to be working with the HTML pane for now, so make sure you're comfortable and have plenty of space.

3 **Type the following basic HTML template into the HTML pane:**

```html
<html>
  <head>
    <title>HTML Template</title>
  </head>
  <body>
    <h1>A basic HTML template</h1>
  </body>
</html>
```

As soon as you type <html>, you get a warning message from JSFiddle, as shown in Figure 3-4, telling you that <html> is already included in the output. What's happening is that JSFiddle knows that every HTML document must have an html element and a head element, so it automatically puts it in there for you. JSFiddle only cares about what comes in between the <body> and </body> tags.

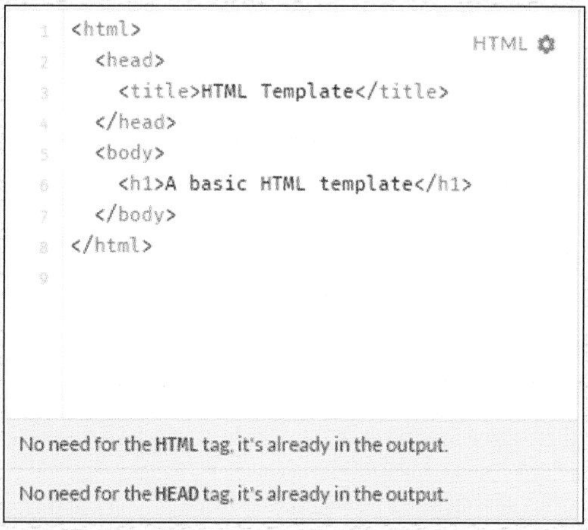

```html
1  <html>                              HTML ⚙
2    <head>
3      <title>HTML Template</title>
4    </head>
5    <body>
6      <h1>A basic HTML template</h1>
7    </body>
8  </html>
9
```

No need for the **HTML** tag, it's already in the output.

No need for the **HEAD** tag, it's already in the output.

Figure 3-4: JSFiddle shows a warning.

4 **Because JSFiddle already includes the basic HTML template, go ahead and delete the** html **tags, the** head **tags, and the** body **tags.**

Always keep in mind that the <html>, <head>, *and* <body> *elements should be part of every HTML document, even if you don't need to type them yourself when you're working in JSFiddle.*

5 **Click Run.**

The text between the <h1> and </h1> tags will display in the Result pane, formatted as a first-level heading, as shown in Figure 3-5.

```
<h1>
A basic HTML template
</h1>
```
                                                HTML ⚙   CSS ⚙

A basic HTML template

                                            JAVASCRIPT ⚙

Figure 3-5: Running the basic HTML template in JSFiddle.

KNOWING YOUR HTML ELEMENTS

HTML has a *lot* of elements. We don't have the space to talk about all the HTML elements here, but we'll cover just enough of them to allow you to build an awesome robot.

There are some really good books on HTML, such as Beginning HTML5 & CSS3 For Dummies, by Ed Tittel and Chris Minnick (Wiley). You can also find a complete list of every HTML element online. Our favorite free online resource is at https://developer.mozilla.org/en-US/docs/Web/HTML/Element.

Table 3-1 lists the most commonly used HTML elements, along with descriptions of what they're used for.

TABLE 3-1 THE MOST COMMON HTML ELEMENTS

Element	Name	Description
`<h1>` through `<h6>`	Heading levels 1 through 6	The heading for a section
`<p>`	Paragraph	A paragraph
`<em>`	Emphasis	Adds emphasis to word(s), often displayed as *italics*
`<strong>`	Strong	Adds strong importance, usually displayed as **bold**
`<a>`	Anchor	A link
`<ul>`	Unordered list	A bulleted list
`<ol>`	Ordered list	A numbered list
`<li>`	List item	An item in an unordered or ordered list
`<img>`	Image	An image
`<hr>`	Horizontal rule	A horizontal line on a page
`<div>`	Division	A way to separate a document into different parts

INTRODUCING DOUGLAS THE ROBOT

We'd like to introduce you to a good friend of ours. His name is Douglas the Robot. He enjoys programming, helping people, and especially dancing.

Douglas the Robot was named after one of our computer programming heroes, Douglas Crockford, who has taught us a lot about programming in general and about programming with JavaScript in particular. Figure 3-6 is a picture of Douglas the Robot.

I <3 JS!

Figure 3-6: Douglas the Robot.

Figure 3-7 is a picture of Douglas Crockford.

Can you see any resemblance?

You'll use HTML to make your basic robot skeleton.

The job of HTML is to give structure to a web page, in the same way that it's the job of your bones to give your body structure.

Go to http://jsfiddle.net/watzthis/zppk3xe2. Notice that there is already some code in the CSS pane. This code is there to make your robot visible.

Photograph courtesy of Robert Claypool
(https://commons.wikimedia.org/wiki/File:
Douglas_Crockford,_February_2013.jpg)

Figure 3-7: Douglas Crockford, JavaScript extraordinaire.

The job of CSS is to give style to HTML.

Without this CSS, Douglas certainly wouldn't look much like a robot. In Chapter 4, after we finish building his skeleton, we'll show you how this CSS code works, and you'll make changes to it to personalize your own version of Douglas.

For now, let's get started with the robot construction!

Follow these steps:

1 **Type the starting tag for the robot's head in the HTML pane.**

```
<div id="robot">
```

2 **Press Return (Mac) or Enter (Windows) several times to create blank lines.**

JS Fiddle automatically puts in the closing `</div>` tag for you. Thanks, JSFiddle!

HTML elements are pretty powerful just by themselves, and they can make web browsers do some pretty fancy things. HTML has some other tricks up its sleeve: HTML attributes! HTML attributes are a way to give web browsers more information about your elements. The id *attribute is used to give your element a unique name; in other words, it identifies it. The* class *attribute, which you'll also be using to build Douglas, identifies a group of elements.*

3 **Between the starting and ending robot** div **tags, type these starting and ending tags to create the robot's head element:**

```
<div id="head">
</div>
```

4 **Between the beginning and ending tags of the head** div **element you just typed, make four new elements for the robot's eyes, nose, and mouth, like this:**

```
<div class="eye" id="righteye"></div>
<div class="eye" id="lefteye"></div>
<div id="nose"></div>
<div id="mouth"></div>
```

Your HTML pane should now have the following code inside it:

```
<div id="robot">
<div id="head">
    <div class="eye" id="righteye"></div>
    <div class="eye" id="lefteye"></div>
    <div id="nose"></div>
    <div id="mouth"></div>
</div>
</div>
```

Notice that we put spaces before the eyes, nose, and mouth elements. We did this so that it's easy to see that the eyes, nose, and mouth are all inside of the head element. Putting spaces at the beginning of lines of code to make them easier to read is called indenting.

TIP

When you put code between the starting and ending tags of other elements, it's called nesting.

REMEMBER

5 **Click Run to see what you have so far.**

You should now see Douglas's head (see Figure 3-8).

Now let's give Douglas a body and two arms!

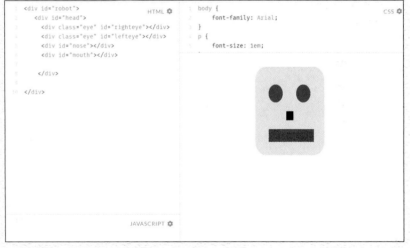

```
<div id="robot">                          HTML ⚙
    <div id="head">
        <div class="eye" id="righteye"></div>
        <div class="eye" id="lefteye"></div>
        <div id="nose"></div>
        <div id="mouth"></div>

    </div>

</div>
```

```
body {                                     CSS ⚙
    font-family: Arial;
}
p {
    font-size: 1em;
}
```

JAVASCRIPT ⚙

Figure 3-8: Creating Douglas's head.

6 **Under the closing** `</div>` **tag of the** head **element, but before the closing tag for the whole robot, create a right arm with this code:**

```
<div class="arm" id="rightarm"></div>
```

7 **Under the right arm, type this code to create Douglas's body:**

```
<div id="body"></div>
```

8 **Under the** body **element, type this last element to create the left arm:**

```
<div class="arm" id="leftarm"></div>
```

9 **Click Run to see the result.**

Douglas now has a head, a face, two arms, and a body, as you can see in Figure 3-9.

Next, we'll write the code to display a message on Douglas's shirt.

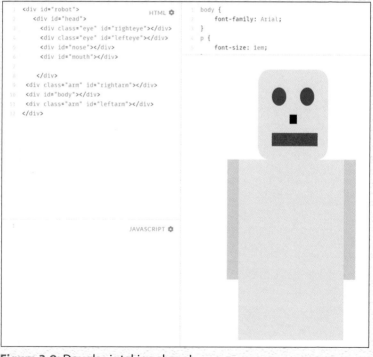

Figure 3-9: Douglas is taking shape!

10 **In between the starting and ending tags for his body, type the following code to display a message:**

```
<p id="message">I Love to Code!</p>
```

11 **Click Run to see the message appear proudly across Douglas's chest, as shown in Figure 3-10.**

Figure 3-10: Douglas wearing a cool T-shirt!

Your finished HTML should look like this:

```
<div id="robot">
<div id="head">
    <div class="eye" id="righteye"></div>
    <div class="eye" id="lefteye"></div>
    <div id="nose"></div>
    <div id="mouth"></div>
</div>
<div class="arm" id="rightarm"></div>
<div id="body"><p id="message">I Love to
    Code!</p></div>
<div class="arm" id="leftarm"></div>
</div>
```

CHANGING HTML USING JAVASCRIPT

Douglas the Robot is pretty cool already, but we want to be able to interact with him and give him commands to make him do things. JavaScript makes it possible to program Douglas to respond to your commands.

Let's write some code to change the message on Douglas's shirt dynamically, using JavaScript!

1 **Type the following into the JavaScript pane:**

```
var myMess = prompt("What should my shirt say?");
document.getElementById("message")
    .innerHTML=myMess;
```

The final code should look like Figure 3-11.

```
    <div id="robot">                              HTML ⚙
        <div id="head">
            <div class="eye" id="righteye"></div>
            <div class="eye" id="lefteye"></div>
            <div id="nose"></div>
            <div id="mouth"></div>
        </div>
    <div class="arm" id="rightarm"></div>
    <div id="body">
        <p id="message">I Love to Code!</p>
    </div>
    <div class="arm" id="leftarm"></div>
    </div>
```

```
                                          JAVASCRIPT ⚙

var myMess = prompt("What should my shirt say?");
document.getElementById("message")
    .innerHTML=myMess;
```

Figure 3-11: The final code for Douglas the Robot.

2 **Click Run.**

A popup window appears, asking you to type in a new message.

3 Type whatever you'd like to display on Douglas's shirt and click OK.

Your new message will appear on Douglas's shirt. We typed a message to show the world what Douglas loves to do (see Figure 3-12)!

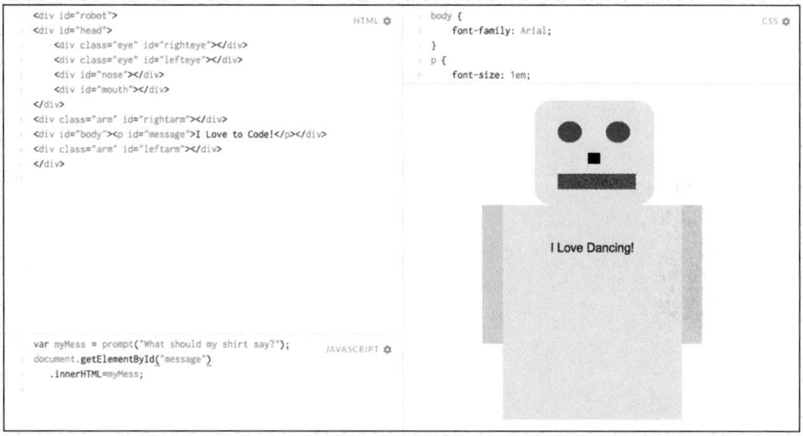

Figure 3-12: Changing Douglas's message.

Now let's take a closer look at this JavaScript code:

```
var myMess = prompt("What should my shirt say?");
document.getElementById("message")
  .innerHTML=myMess;
```

This code is made up of two statements. This first statement tells JavaScript to ask you a question. Another name for a question is a prompt.

```
var myMess = prompt("What should my shirt say?");
```

After you've answered this question, your answer gets put into your variable, `var myMess`, where it will be stored and used by the next statement.

The next statement has a command:

```
getElementById
```

The job of this command is to look at the HTML and find an element by its unique ID. In this case, it's looking for the element with the ID of `message`.

```
getElementById("message")
```

This command searches and finds this HTML element:

```
<p id="message">I love to Code!</p>
```

The next command tells JavaScript that we want to change the HTML and what to change it to:

```
.innerHTML=myMess
```

The "inner" HTML is this part of the HTML element:

```
I Love to Code!
```

SUMMARY

In this chapter, you used HTML to create the basic body structure of Douglas the Robot and you learned how to use JavaScript to make alerts you can interact with. In the next chapter, you'll learn how to give your robot a unique style using CSS.

PROJECT 4 GIVING YOUR ROBOT STYLE

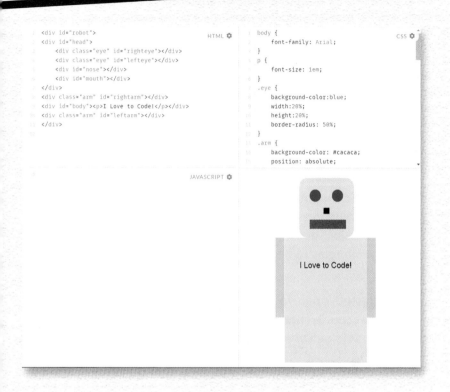

```
<div id="robot">                                    HTML ⚙
<div id="head">
    <div class="eye" id="righteye"></div>
    <div class="eye" id="lefteye"></div>
    <div id="nose"></div>
    <div id="mouth"></div>
</div>
<div class="arm" id="rightarm"></div>
<div id="body"><p>I Love to Code!</p></div>
<div class="arm" id="leftarm"></div>
</div>
```

```
body {                                               CSS ⚙
    font-family: Arial;
}
p {
    font-size: 1em;
}
.eye {
    background-color:blue;
    width:20%;
    height:20%;
    border-radius: 50%;
}
.arm {
    background-color: #cacaca;
    position: absolute;
```

JAVASCRIPT ⚙

I Love to Code!

EVERYONE HAS HIS OR HER OWN INDIVIDUAL STYLE. Your style might be similar to your best friend's style, or it might be totally different. You may feel most comfortable in jeans and a T-shirt, and your best friend might prefer being dressed up. Styles also come and go: What's in style today might look silly ten years from now. If you don't believe us, ask your parents to see a photograph of what they looked like in high school. When you're done laughing, read on.

You can change the way you look by changing your clothes. But what makes you who you are, doesn't change when you change your clothes. In the same way, it's possible to change the way HTML looks without changing its content and structure.

» **Declaration block:** The declaration block contains one or more CSS declarations, which indicate how to style the selected element(s). In this example, we have just one declaration: `font-family: Arial;`. This declaration will change the look, or font, of all the text that appears in the Result pane.

The HTML body element is where everything that will display in your document goes. Even though you don't need to type it into JSFiddle, it's still there, because JSFiddle puts it into the Result pane for you.

CSS SELECTORS

The selector is the part of the CSS rule that comes before the {. CSS selectors tell the web browser which HTML elements a style should apply to.

The official name for the { and } characters are curly braces or curly brackets. You can also call them mustaches, though, because they look like fancy mustaches turned on their sides. Figure 4-2 shows Douglas sporting a curly brace mustache.

I Love My Mustache!

Figure 4-2: Douglas demonstrating that curly braces look like mustaches.

When you select an element to apply a style to, that same style is applied to every element inside the selected element.

CSS selectors have a number of different ways to select elements. Let's look at three of these while working with Douglas the Robot:

» **Element selectors:** Take a look at the first two rules in the CSS panel:

```
body {
    font-family: Arial;
}
p {
    font-size: 1em;
}
```

These are both examples of element selectors. Element selectors select HTML elements using the name of the element.

To use an element selector, just type the name of the element you want to select. In these cases, we're selecting the body element (which uses <body> and </body> tags) and the p element (which uses <p> and </p> tags).

» **Class selectors:** Class selectors are ideal for times when you need to apply the same style to multiple elements.

You can think of them like a class in school — many kids are all in the same class and that class has a name (like History or Math). All the students in the class are unique, but they're all learning the same subject because they're all part of the same class.

Now take a look at the third CSS rule in the JavaScript CSS pane:

```
.eye {
    background-color: blue;
    width: 20%;
    height: 20%;
    border-radius: 50%;
}
```

The class selector starts with a period (.), followed by the name of the class.

In this case, we're selecting all the elements that have `class="eye"`. If you look in the HTML pane, you can see that there are two elements with `class="eye"`. These are used to make Douglas's two eyes.

When you put text like `something="something"` *inside a starting tag in HTML, that's called an* attribute. *For example, in the tag* `<p class="myText">`, `class` *is an attribute and its value is* `myText`.

The same style is applied to both of Douglas's eyes. They're both blue, and they're the same size (see Figure 4-3).

Figure 4-3: Douglas's eyes are styled with class selectors.

» **ID selectors:** The `id` attribute of an HTML element is how you can uniquely identify an element. Think of an `id` attribute as being like an element's name. If your teacher wants to call on a single student in your class, she can do that by using the student's name. Using an ID selector works the same way.

Douglas has two eyes, which you know are both part of the `"eye"` class. But we also need to be able to style, move, blink, and wink his eyes separately. To make this possible, we gave each eye its own unique name. The right eye is called (appropriately enough) `"righteye"` and the left eye is called `"lefteye"`, as you can see in the HTML for his eyes:

```
<div class="eye" id="righteye"></div>
<div class="eye" id="lefteye"></div>
```

ID selectors start with a hash symbol (#) and select elements using the element's unique name, or ID attribute.

For example, Douglas's left eye and right eye have separate ID attributes (see Figure 4-4).

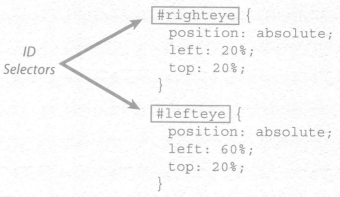

```
#righteye {
    position: absolute;
    left: 20%;
    top: 20%;
}
```

ID Selectors

```
#lefteye {
    position: absolute;
    left: 60%;
    top: 20%;
}
```

Figure 4-4: Douglas's eyes have separate IDs.

ID selectors are useful when you need to select a single element in an HTML document.

Every ID attribute must be unique within your HTML page.

Table 4-1 is a handy guide to everything you need to know about CSS selectors and how to use them.

TABLE 4-1 THE BASICS OF CSS SELECTORS

Selector Name	Selector Symbol	Example
element	(none)	`p {}` selects `<p></p>`
class	. (period)	`.red{}` selects `<p class="red"></p>`
id	#	`#best{}` selects `<p id="best"></p>`

Now that you know how to select what element or elements you want to style, let's talk about how to go about styling them and all the great things you can do with CSS declarations.

CSS DECLARATIONS

CSS declarations go inside the curly braces following CSS selectors. Each declaration must end with a semicolon (;). You can have as many declarations between the curly braces as you need to get the job done.

Declarations are made up of two parts:

» **Property:** The property part of a declaration tells what should be modified. For example, you can change the color, width, or location of an element.

   CSS contains many different properties, and we'll show you how to use some of them shortly!

   The property must be followed by a colon (:).

» **Value:** The value tells how the property should be changed. For example, you might change the color of Douglas's nose to red. In this example, `color` is the property, and `red` is the value.

To see how declarations work, let's take a look into Douglas's eye styles. For the `eye` class, we created four declarations:

```
.eye {
    background-color:blue;
    width:20%;
    height:20%;
    border-radius: 50%;
}
```

Each of these four declarations changes something about Douglas's eyes.

Figure 4-5 shows each part of a CSS rule.

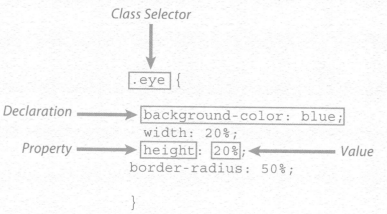

Class Selector

`.eye` {

Declaration ⟶ `background-color: blue;`
`width: 20%;`
Property ⟶ `height` : `20%` ; ⟵ *Value*
`border-radius: 50%;`

}

Figure 4-5: Dissecting a CSS rule.

The word on the left is called the property, *and the word on the right is called the* value.

Let's look at some CSS properties now.

CSS PROPERTIES

CSS properties change the characteristics of elements. Douglas the Robot's beautiful eye color, the size of his body and arms, the roundness of the corners of his head, and the position of his different parts are all determined by the values of those properties.

Let's make some changes to Douglas's looks by modifying the values of some different CSS properties:

1 In the CSS pane, find the CSS rule for the p **element.**

It's currently the second rule in the CSS pane.

2 Change the value of the font-size **property to** 2.5em.

The complete rule should now look like this:

```
p {
  font-size: 2.5em;
}
```

There are several different ways to say how big text should be. The most commonly used ways are by using pixels (px), percent (%), or ems (em). The bigger the number before the px, %, or em, the bigger the text will be. For example, 2.5em is two and a half times bigger than 1em.

3 Click the Run button to see the change in the Result pane.

The text on Douglas's shirt is now bigger.

4 Find the CSS rule for the body **element.**

5 Change the value of the body **element to the following, paying attention to the use of quotes:**

```
"Comic Sans MS", cursive, sans-serif
```

The complete CSS rule should now look like this:

```
body {
    font-family: "Comic Sans MS", cursive,
    sans-serif;
}
```

6 Click the Run button to see the results.

Douglas now has interesting letters on his shirt, as shown in Figure 4-6.

Next, let's change Douglas's eye color to match your eye color!

Figure 4-6: Douglas, now with fun letters!

7 Find the CSS rule that contains Douglas's eye color.

It currently looks like this:

```
.eye {
    background-color:blue;
    width: 20%;
    height: 20%;
    border-radius: 50%;
}
```

8 Change the value of the `background-color` **property to your eye color.**

For example, if your eyes are brown, you would change it to the following:

```
background-color: brown;
```

9 **Click the Run button to see the results.**

Our CSS pane with the changes made should look similar to Figure 4-7.

```
1  body {                                           CSS ⚙
2      font-family: "Comic Sans MS", cursive,
3      sans-serif;
4  }
5  p {
6      font-size: 2.5em;
7  }
8  .eye {
9      background-color:brown;
10     width:20%;
11     height:20%;
12     border-radius: 50%;
13 }
14 .arm {
```

Figure 4-7: CSS styles give Douglas the Robot brown eyes.

Notice that the color that Douglas's eyes change to when you use the word *brown* doesn't look very realistic, and the color that is used when you try to make Douglas's eyes green also isn't a color that anyone's eyes are likely to be. To get a more precise color, check out the next section.

COLORIZING DOUGLAS

CSS lets you use millions of different colors. In this section, we'll explore the vast universe of colors that are available to you.

USING CSS COLORS

CSS colors use different combinations of red, green, and blue to describe the millions of possible colors that a web browser can display.

Some colors can be named using color words. These include the names that you're familiar with such as red, blue, pink, and yellow. There are also more exotic and interesting colors available, and they have names like HoneyDew, HotPink, and LemonChiffon (yum!).

Even the full list of color names in CSS doesn't come close to describing every color you might want to use. Fortunately, CSS also lets us specify colors using a code called *RGB notation*. RGB notation uses different amounts of red, green, and blue to make every possible color. RGB colors are made up of three numbers, ranging from 0 to 255. The color red is made up of all red, no green, and no blue, so it's written as (255,0,0). The color black is made up of no color at all, so it's written as (0,0,0). The color blue is all blue, no red, and no green, and its RGB code is (0,0,255). Can you figure out how to make purple?

Table 4-2 lists some color names you can use in HTML, as well as their RGB codes.

TABLE 4-2 STANDARD COLOR NAMES

Color Name	RGB Value	Color Swatch
Aqua	(0,255,255)	
Black	(0,0,0)	
Blue	(0,0,255)	
Fuchsia	(255,0,255)	
Gray	(128,128,128)	
Green	(0,255,0)	

(continued)

TABLE 4-2 (CONTINUED)

Color Name	RGB Value	Color Swatch
Lime	(0,255,0)	
Maroon	(128,0,0)	
Navy	(0,0,128)	
Olive	(0,0,128)	
Orange	(255,165,0)	
Purple	(128,0,128)	
Red	(255,0,0)	
Silver	(192,192,192)	
Teal	(0,128,128)	
White	(255,255,255)	
Yellow	(255,255,0)	

For a complete list of all the color names and RGB codes, visit
www.rapidtables.com/web/color/RGB_Color.htm. When you get
there, you'll see a table near the bottom of the page with a long
list of colors. Figure 4-8 shows just the beginning of this table.

Color	Color Name	Hex Code #RRGGBB	Decimal Code R,G,B
	maroon	#800000	(128,0,0)
	dark red	#8B0000	(139,0,0)
	brown	#A52A2A	(165,42,42)
	firebrick	#B22222	(178,34,34)
	crimson	#DC143C	(220,20,60)
	red	#FF0000	(255,0,0)
	tomato	#FF6347	(255,99,71)
	coral	#FF7F50	(255,127,80)
	indian red	#CD5C5C	(205,92,92)
	light coral	#F08080	(240,128,128)
	dark salmon	#E9967A	(233,150,122)
	salmon	#FA8072	(250,128,114)
	light salmon	#FFA07A	(255,160,122)
	orange red	#FF4500	(255,69,0)
	dark orange	#FF8C00	(255,140,0)
	orange	#FFA500	(255,165,0)
	gold	#FFD700	(255,215,0)

Figure 4-8: The beginning of the complete table of named colors.

If you look at the CSS color table in Figure 4-8, or if you examine certain parts of Douglas's CSS, you'll also see another way to make colors in CSS. This third method uses letters and numbers that start with a hash symbol (#). This method is called hexadecimal notation.

CHANGING COLORS

Now let's use our new color knowledge to make some changes to Douglas's different parts.

You already played around with changing the color of Douglas's eyes. What about changing the color of his mouth? In the CSS pane, find the ID selector and declaration for Douglas's mouth. It looks like this:

```
#mouth {
    position: absolute;
    width: 65%;
```

```
    height: 15%;
    left: 20%;
    top: 70%;
    background-color: red;
}
```

Right now, you have the color for Douglas's mouth set to the color red. To use one of the RGB colors in Table 4-1, you first need to tell the program that you're using an RGB color; then add the RGB code of the color you want to use. If you wanted to change the color of Douglas's mouth to teal, you would write it like this:

```
#mouth {
    position: absolute;
    width: 65%;
    height: 15%;
    left: 20%;
    top: 70%;
    background-color: rgb(0,128,128);
}
```

The result is shown in Figure 4-9.

Try changing the color of Douglas's mouth in your own CSS pane.

Directly above the mouth declaration block, there is the declaration block for Douglas's nose. You can change the color of Douglas's nose in much the same way as you changed his mouth:

```
#nose {
    position: absolute;
    left: 45%;
    top: 50%;
    width: 10%;
    height: 10%;
    background-color: rgb(255,0,0);
}
```

The result is shown in Figure 4-10.

Next let's change Douglas's shirt body color. Find the declaration block for his body, and change it to any color you'd like! For example, here's how to change it to yellow:

```
#mouth {
    position: absolute;
    width: 65%;
    height: 15%;
    left: 20%;
    top: 70%;
    background-color: rgb(0,128,128);
}
```

Figure 4-9: Douglas with a teal-colored mouth.

```
#nose {
    position: absolute;
    left: 45%;
    top: 50%;
    width: 10%;
    height: 10%;
    background-color: rgb(255,0,0);
}
```

Figure 4-10: Douglas the red-nosed robot.

```
#body {
    position: absolute;
    left: 25%;
    top: 35%;
    width: 45%;
    height: 55%;
    background-color: rgb(255,255,0);
    text-align:center;
    padding-top: 30px;
}
```

The result is shown in Figure 4-11.

Figure 4-11: Making Douglas's shirt yellow.

CUSTOMIZING YOUR OWN ROBOT

Now it's your turn! See how many of the following CSS challenges
you can complete.

In order to figure out the color codes for some of these, use the online color chart at www.rapidtables.com/web/color/RGB_Color.htm.

» Make Douglas's left arm blue.

» Make Douglas's right arm medium sea green.

» Change the color of the message on Douglas's shirt to white, and make his shirt black.

» Make the size of the message on Douglas's shirt larger.

Figure 4-12 shows what our robot looked like after we made all these changes!

What does yours look like? If you want to share him with us or with your friends, just click Update to save your fiddle and then copy the web address and send it!

SUMMARY

In this chapter, you learned how to use CSS to change the style of HTML elements and you learned how to resize and position elements using CSS. In the next chapter, you'll learn how to make Douglas dance!

```
body {                                              CSS ⚙
    font-family: "Comic Sans MS", cursive, sans-serif;;
}
p {
    font-size: 3em;
    color: rgb(255,255,255);
}
.eye {
    background-color:brown;
    width:20%;
    height:20%;
    border-radius: 50%;
```

Figure 4-12: The style we designed for Douglas.

PROJECT 5 ANIMATING YOUR ROBOT

```javascript
document.getElementById("lefteye")
    .style.backgroundColor = "purple";
document.getElementById("head")
    .style.transform = "rotate(15deg)";
```

JAVASCRIPT ⚙

I Love
to Code!

IN CHAPTER 3, YOU LEARNED HOW YOU CAN USE JAVASCRIPT TO CHANGE HTML. You can also use JavaScript to change CSS styles. And the process is very similar.

In this chapter, we'll use CSS and JavaScript to make Douglas dance!

CHANGING CSS WITH JAVASCRIPT

The first step in changing CSS using JavaScript is to locate the element you want to change. In Chapter 3, we showed you how to give an HTML element an `id` attribute and how to locate that unique ID using `getElementById`. For example, to select Douglas's left eye, you can use the following code:

```
document.getElementById("lefteye")
```

This code searches the HTML to locate the element with the ID of `lefteye` that we created in Chapter 3:

```
<div class="eye" id="lefteye"></div>
```

After JavaScript has located the element to change, you tell JavaScript what part of that element you want to change.

In Chapter 3, in order to tell JavaScript to change the HTML, we used `.innerHTML`:

```
document.getElementById("message").innerHTML =
    "Coding is Fun!";
```

The inner HTML of an element is everything between the starting and ending tags.

Just as elements have inner HTML, which you can changing using `.innerHTML`, elements also have style, which you can change using `.style.`:

```
document.getElementById("lefteye").style
```

After you've told JavaScript that that you want to change a style, you need to tell JavaScript what property you want to change.

 CSS properties let you change things like the size, color, font, and position of HTML elements.

To change the background color of Douglas's left eye, you use the `backgroundColor` property:

```
document.getElementById("lefteye")
    .style.backgroundColor
```

You then tell it what the new value of the property should be. To change the style property of `backgroundColor` to the value of `purple`, we use this code:

```
document.getElementById("lefteye")
    .style.backgroundColor = "purple";
```

JavaScript style properties are not always spelled the same as CSS style properties. JavaScript style properties use camelCase capitalization instead of dashes to separate multiple words.

Table 5-1 shows some common CSS properties along with their JavaScript counterparts.

TABLE 5-1 CSS PROPERTIES AND JAVASCRIPT STYLE PROPERTIES

CSS Property	JavaScript Style Property
margin	margin
font-size	fontSize
border-width	borderWidth
text-align	textAlign
color	color

To see a complete list of JavaScript style properties, visit
www.w3schools.com/jsref/dom_obj_style.asp.

MODIFYING DOUGLAS WITH JAVASCRIPT

Modifying CSS using JavaScript makes it possible for the look
and position of elements to change in response to your actions.

We'll make Douglas dance in a little bit, but first let's get some
practice with making style changes to him using JavaScript:

1 **Log into JSFiddle and find the project titled
Chapter 5 – Changing CSS with JS – Start.**

You see the Douglas Robot project pretty much as we left it
at the end of Chapter 3, as shown in Figure 5-1.

2 **Click the Fork button to create a copy of this program in
your own JSFiddle account.**

3 **Type the following into the JavaScript pane to change
Douglas's left eye color:**

```
document.getElementById("lefteye")
    .style.backgroundColor = "purple";
```

Figure 5-1: Douglas, the unanimated JavaScript robot.

4 **Click Run to see the result.**

Douglas's left eye will change to purple, as shown in Figure 5-2.

5 **Press Return (Mac) or Enter (Windows) to start a new line in the JavaScript panel and then type the following:**

```
document.getElementById("head")
    .style.transform = "rotate(15deg)";
```

6 **Click Run to see the result.**

Douglas now is tilting his head to his left, as shown in Figure 5-3. He looks ready to start dancing!

7 **Click Update and then click Set as Base to save your program to your public dashboard.**

```html
<div id="robot">                          HTML ⚙
  <div id="head">
    <div class="eye" id="righteye"></div>
    <div class="eye" id="lefteye"></div>
    <div id="nose"></div>
    <div id="mouth"></div>
  </div>
  <div class="arm" id="rightarm"></div>
  <div id="body"><p id="message">I Love to Code!</p>
  </div>
  <div class="arm" id="leftarm"></div>
</div>
```

```css
body {                                    CSS ⚙
    font-family: "Comic Sans MS", cursive, sans-
serif;
}
p {
    font-size: 3em;
}
.eye {
    background-color:blue;
    width:30%;
    height:30%;
    border-radius: 50%;
```

```javascript
document.getElementById("lefteye")       JAVASCRIPT ⚙
    .style.backgroundColor = "purple";
```

Figure 5-2: Douglas's left eye is now purple.

```javascript
document.getElementById("lefteye")       JAVASCRIPT ⚙
    .style.backgroundColor = "purple";
document.getElementById("head")
    .style.transform = "rotate(15deg)";
```

Figure 5-3: Douglas is ready to dance!

EXPERIMENTING WITH DOUGLAS

There are a lot of possibilities for customizing Douglas using JavaScript's style properties. To get started experimenting with a few, try adding each of the following statements to the JavaScript pane and then running them:

```
// Put a 2-pixel-wide, solid black border around his
   body.
document.getElementById("body")
   .style.border = "2px black solid";

// Round the corners of his mouth.
document.getElementById("mouth")
   .style.borderRadius = "4px";

// Put yellow dots around his right eye.
document.getElementById("righteye")
   .style.border = "4px yellow dotted";

// Change his left arm's color.
document.getElementById("leftarm")
   .style.backgroundColor = "purple";

// Change the text color.
document.getElementById("body")
   .style.color = "red";

// Give Douglas hair.
document.getElementById("head")
   .style.borderTop = "5px black solid";
```

Notice the lines of text that start with // before the JavaScript statements. These are comments. They're there just to tell you (or other programmers) what the JavaScript code does. JavaScript doesn't even look at them. You can use comments in your own code by typing // anywhere you want to leave a note. Everything that follows the // and that is on the same line as them will be ignored.

Figure 5-4 shows what Douglas looks like with all these changes made.

Figure 5-4: Douglas with crazy-looking style changes!

Now it's your turn. Can you figure out how to make each of the following changes using JavaScript? If you need help with any of these, visit our public dashboard on JSFiddle and look for the program named Chapter 5 – Changing CSS with JS – Finished.

» Tilt Douglas's head to the other side.

» Make Douglas's nose round.

» Make Douglas's right arm green.

» Make Douglas's lips pink.

Keep in mind that JavaScript is very sensitive. If you have a typo, or forget a period, or spell getElementById *wrong anywhere in the JavaScript pane, none of the lines of JavaScript will run.*

MAKING DOUGLAS DANCE

Now that you know how to change CSS using JavaScript, let's put that knowledge to good use and make Douglas more animated!

1 Go to https://jsfiddle.net/watzthis/fwdh1gdy and click the Fork button in JSFiddle.

2 Click Fiddle Meta in the left menu to open Fiddle Options.

3 Change the name of the fiddle to *Your Name*'s Animated Robot.

4 Click Update to save your work.

You'll see a new fiddle with some code in each of the three code panes — HTML, CSS, and JavaScript — as shown in Figure 5-5.

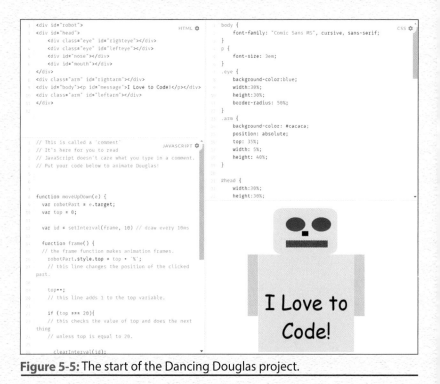

Figure 5-5: The start of the Dancing Douglas project.

Now you have a new fiddle for the new and improved dancing Douglas, and you can still get to the previous, nondancing Douglas from your public dashboard.

Douglas isn't the greatest dancer, but he does have a few moves that he's very proud of. The first is one he calls the "eye bounce." His eye makes a quick movement upward and then floats back into place. Trust us, when he does it to the beat, it's almost hypnotic.

Figure 5-6 shows Douglas in the middle of one of his signature eye bounces.

Figure 5-6: Douglas doing the eye bounce.

In this program, you're going to control Douglas's dancing by clicking his different parts to animate them. We start with programming his right eye to bounce when you click it.

1 **In the JavaScript pane, press Return (Mac) or Enter (Windows) a few times at the top of all the existing code in order to give yourself some space to add your code and type the following statement:**

```
var rightEye = document.getElementById("righteye");
```

This variable declaration creates a shortcut for us to refer to the right eye. Now that this has been created, every time you need to refer to Douglas's right eye in the rest of the program, you can just use the variable named `rightEye`.

2 Tell JavaScript to listen for mouse clicks on the right eye with this statement:

```
rightEye.addEventListener("click", moveUpDown);
```

This statement is what's called an *event listener*. Here's how it works.

First, it locates an element — in this case, the `rightEye`, with the ID of `"righteye"`

```
var rightEye = document.getElementById("righteye");
```

Once it knows what element you're talking about, it adds an event listener to that element. The job of an event listener is to wait until something happens and then take an action. In this case, it's waiting for you to click your mouse on the selected element (`rightEye`).

Once it detects that you've clicked the `rightEye` element, it will take an action. In this case, the action it will take is called `moveUpDown`. We've already created the `moveUpDown` action, which you can see in the JavaScript window.

Another name for an action is function. Just like a toaster has an action it can do (toast bread), Douglas has a function he can do, which is called `moveUpDown`.

Here's the JavaScript code for Douglas's `moveUpDown` function:

```
function moveUpDown(e) {
  var robotPart = e.target;
  var top = 0;

  var id = setInterval(frame, 10) // draw every 10ms
```

```
function frame() {
  robotPart.style.top = top + '%';
  top++;
  if (top === 20){
    clearInterval(id);
  }
 }
}
```

We'll tell you how this function works in a minute, but first let's talk about how animation works.

CREATING ANIMATIONS WITH JAVASCRIPT

Computer animation, like film and video animation, is a trick. The trick is to show a series of pictures very quickly so that the images appear to move.

Some of the very first uses of animation were called flipbooks or kineographs (see Figure 5-7), and they first became popular in 1886. Flipbooks are made by drawing a slightly different picture near the edge of each page of a notebook or a stack of springy pieces of paper. You can then flip through the book to see a cartoon.

If you have a stack of index cards or a notebook, you can make your own flipbook. Figure 5-8 shows a picture of a flipbook animation that we made of Douglas the Robot dancing.

Today's animation works the same way as flipbooks, but we use computers and programming to create each picture instead of stacks of paper.

Each single picture in an animation is called a *frame*. The way Douglas's eye-bounce animation works is by showing his eye in a slightly different place, every 10 milliseconds (one-tenth of a second). When you click his eye, it jumps to the top of his head and floats back down to its starting point.

THE KINEOGRAPH.

Figure 5-7: An early form of animation.

Source: https://commons.wikimedia.org/wiki/File%3ALinnet_kineograph_1886.jpg

Figure 5-8: Our flipbook animation of Douglas the Robot dancing.

Figure 5-9 shows the position of the eye at various points during the animation.

Figure 5-9: Douglas's eye at various points in the animation.

Now let's look closely at the code for the `moveUpDown` function and see how it's created. The first line gives the function its name:

```
function moveUpDown(e) {
```

The next line creates a statement that finds out what part of the robot (or element) you clicked:

```
var robotPart = e.target;
```

It stores the information about that element in a new variable called `robotPart`.

This next statement creates a new variable called `top` and gives it a value of 0:

```
var top = 0;
```

This `top` variable is what we use to change the position of the eye in each frame of the animation.

The following line uses a command called `setInterval` to make the animation happen:

```
var id = setInterval(frame, 10);
```

The `setInterval` command makes JavaScript do something repeatedly. How fast it does the repeated action is set using a number — in this case, the number 10.

This number is the number of milliseconds (thousandths of a second) to wait before doing the thing again. One thousand milliseconds equals one second. The larger this number is, the slower the animation will appear to be moving.

Next, we create a new function that belongs to Douglas's `moveUpDown` function. The purpose of this new function is to create each frame of the animation, so we call the function frame:

```
function frame() {
```

If you'd like to look at the frame function in more depth, visit https://jsfiddle.net/watzthis/fwdh1gdy and read the comments inside the JavaScript pane.

ANIMATING ANOTHER ELEMENT

Now that we've written the `moveUpDown` function to animate one eye, animating the other eye is a simple matter of adding another event listener.

1 **Click Update to save your work so far.**

2 **Type the following new variable declaration just below the one for** `rightEye`**:**

```
var leftEye = document.getElementById("lefteye");
```

3 **Type a new event listener just below the event listener for the** `rightEye` **one:**

```
leftEye.addEventListener("click", moveUpDown);
```

4 **Click Run.**

Now, clicking either the left eye or the right eye will cause the `moveUpDown` animation to happen on the clicked element.

USING A SECOND ANIMATION FUNCTION

Douglas has at least one more dance move besides the eye bounce. He calls this one the "arm sweep." This classic move involves a smooth movement of the left arm from the right to the left across Douglas's body as his eyes stare straight ahead.

Before we create the arm sweep animation, we'll make a couple CSS changes so that Douglas's left arm is extended, rather than just hanging at his side.

1 **In the CSS pane, locate the style block for the left arm. It looks like this:**

```
#leftarm {
    position: absolute;
    left: 70%;
}
```

2 **Add a new** width **property and a** height **property to the left arm styles. Set the** width **to 30% and set the** height **to 7%.**

The finished leftarm styles will now look like this:

```
#leftarm {
    position: absolute;
    left: 70%;
    width: 30%;
    height: 7%;
}
```

3 **Click Run, and Douglas's arm will point out to the side (see Figure 5-10).**

Now you're ready to create the arm sweep animation. To create the arm sweep animation, we'll add a third event listener.

1 **Create a new variable, just under the two other variables, to represent the left arm:**

```
var leftArm = document.getElementById("leftarm");
```

2 **Write a new event listener, underneath the two other event listeners:**

```
leftArm.addEventListener("click", moveRightLeft);
```

```
#leftarm {
    position: absolute;
    left: 70%;
    width: 30%;
    height: 7%;
}
```

I Love to Code!

Figure 5-10: Douglas is pointing and ready to do the arm sweep.

This new event listener will watch for you to click Douglas's left arm, and then it will make him to do the `moveRightLeft` action (or function).

We've already written the `moveRightLeft` function for you. It works pretty much the same as the `moveUpDown` function, but we modified it slightly in order to animate the arm from right to left instead of from top to bottom.

Here's Douglas's `moveRightLeft` function:

```
function moveRightLeft(e) {
  var robotPart = e.target;
  var left = 0;
  var id = setInterval(frame, 10) // draw every 10ms
  function frame() {
    robotPart.style.left = left + '%';
    left++;
    if (left === 70){
      clearInterval(id);
    }
  }
}
```

To save your work and test out the new animation, click
Update. When you click Douglas's left arm now, you'll see the
moveRightLeft animation work.

The completed code in the JavaScript pane should now match
the following:

```javascript
var rightEye = document.getElementById("righteye");
var leftEye = document.getElementById("lefteye");
var leftArm = document.getElementById("leftarm");

rightEye.addEventListener("click", moveUpDown);
leftEye.addEventListener("click", moveUpDown);
leftArm.addEventListener("click", moveRightLeft);

function moveUpDown(e) {
  var robotPart = e.target;
  var top = 0;
  var id = setInterval(frame, 10) // draw every 10ms
  function frame() {
    robotPart.style.top = top + '%';
    top++;
    if (top === 20){
      clearInterval(id);
    }
  }
}


function moveRightLeft(e) {
  var robotPart = e.target;
  var left = 0;
  var id = setInterval(frame, 10) // draw every 10ms
  function frame() {
    robotPart.style.left = left + '%';
    left++;
    if (left === 70){
      clearInterval(id);
    }
  }
}
```

Now it's your turn to have some fun making Douglas dance! Start out by turning on some music and clicking his eyes and arm to the beat! Next, try adding some new event listeners to animate different parts of Douglas, such as his nose, his mouth, or his right arm!

SUMMARY

In this chapter, you used all the tools you learned in the previous chapters, plus some brand-new ones, to make your animated robot dance. This is only the beginning of what you can do with HTML, CSS, and JavaScript. Keep exploring and playing and be sure to email us at `info@watzthis.com` if you have questions or want to share your creations with us.

PROJECT 6 CREATING A JAVASCRIPT WORD GAME

fluffy
ADJECTIVE

practicing
VERB (ENDING IN "ING")

dining room
ROOM IN A HOUSE

blue
COLOR

tooth brushes
PLURAL NOUN

threw
VERB (PAST TENSE)

milk
BEVERAGE

Douglas's Dance Party

One FLUFFY day, Douglas was PRACTICING in his DINING ROOM, reading a book about BLUE TOOTH BRUSHES.

As he THREW his MILK, he heard SMOOTH JAZZ music playing in the BATHROOM.

WOW! he exclaimed, as he ROLLED down the stairs to join the GOOFY party.

Douglas danced the SHARK Dance, the BELGRADE Shake, and took the prize for dancing the best Electric LIFT.

WORD REPLACEMENT GAMES GIVE YOU A BASIC STORY AND ASK PLAYERS TO FILL IN THE DIFFERENT PARTS, SUCH AS NOUNS, VERBS, ADJECTIVES, AND SO ON. We use HTML, CSS, and JavaScript code to create the basic skeleton of the story. The variables in the JavaScript code are what make the results of the program different every time it's run.

CREATING A VARIABLE STORY

To create this game, we wrote a story about Douglas the JavaScript Robot's adventures. Then we removed some of the words so that the person playing the game can fill them in.

Here's our story about Douglas the JavaScript Robot, with certain words removed and replaced with the type of word the program needs from the player (underlined):

One underlined adjective day, Douglas was underlined verb ending in "–ing" in his underlined room in house, reading a book about underlined color underlined plural noun.

As he past-tense verb his beverage, he heard type of music music playing in the different room in house.

exclamation! he exclaimed, as he past-tense verb down the stairs to join the adjective party.

Douglas danced the name of animal Dance, the name of city Twist, and took the prize for dancing the best Electric verb.

Now that we have the story, let's build a JavaScript program around it that will accept input from a user and output a customized — and hilarious — story.

CREATING THE WORD REPLACEMENT GAME

The word replacement game makes use of everything you've learned in this book, including variables, operators, event handlers, HTML, CSS, input, output, and more!

Before we jump into the building of the game, let's try it out and see it in action:

1 **Open your web browser and go to our JSFiddle Public Dashboard at https://jsfiddle.net/user/watzthis.**

2 **Locate the fiddle named Chapter 6 – Word Game, and click the title to open it.**

The finished word game project will open up.

3 **Depending on your screen size, you may need to adjust the size of the Result pane so that it fits correctly.**

You should see a very short rectangle with a dotted border to the right of the input questions. This is where the finished story will display.

4 **Click the underline right above the first question to select the text input field.**

5 Enter a word in the input field.

After you've entered the word you like, press the Tab key or use your mouse to click the next input field on the page and fill that one out.

6 When you've finished filling out all the fields, click the Replace It button at the bottom of the form.

The story of Douglas's adventure appears on the right with the words you entered into the input fields inserted, as shown in Figure 6-1.

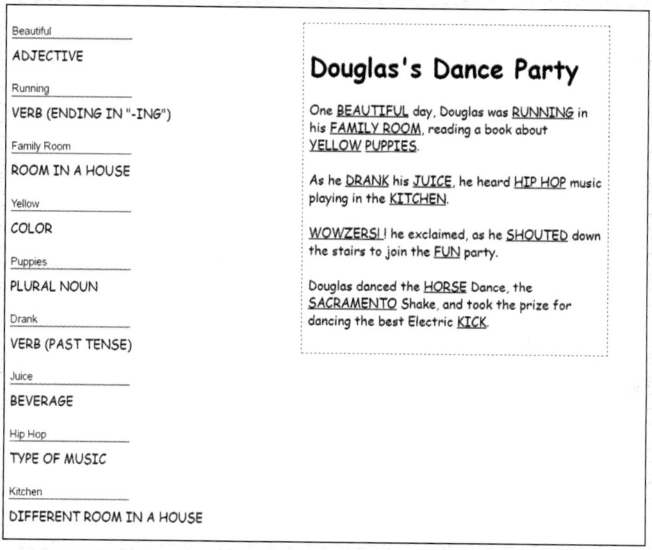

Beautiful
ADJECTIVE

Running
VERB (ENDING IN "-ING")

Family Room
ROOM IN A HOUSE

Yellow
COLOR

Puppies
PLURAL NOUN

Drank
VERB (PAST TENSE)

Juice
BEVERAGE

Hip Hop
TYPE OF MUSIC

Kitchen
DIFFERENT ROOM IN A HOUSE

Douglas's Dance Party

One BEAUTIFUL day, Douglas was RUNNING in his FAMILY ROOM, reading a book about YELLOW PUPPIES.

As he DRANK his JUICE, he heard HIP HOP music playing in the KITCHEN.

WOWZERS! he exclaimed, as he SHOUTED down the stairs to join the FUN party.

Douglas danced the HORSE Dance, the SACRAMENTO Shake, and took the prize for dancing the best Electric KICK.

Figure 6-1: The finished story of Douglas's adventure.

Now that you've seen how the program works, let's start from scratch and build it. When you know how to build the game, you'll be able to add to it, improve it, and even change the story completely!

7 **Type the third `<div>` element underneath all the other markup in the HTML pane.**

```
<div id="story"></div>
```

If you've entered everything correctly, your HTML pane should now look like the following:

```
<div id="inputWords">
  <ul>
    <li><input type="text" id="adj1"><br>Adjective
  </li>
<!-- put other input fields here -->

  </ul>
<div id="buttonDiv"></div>
</div>
<div id="story"></div>
```

8 **Click Run to see what your word game looks like so far.**

It should look like Figure 6-2.

The final step that we'll do in the HTML pane for now is to create the button.

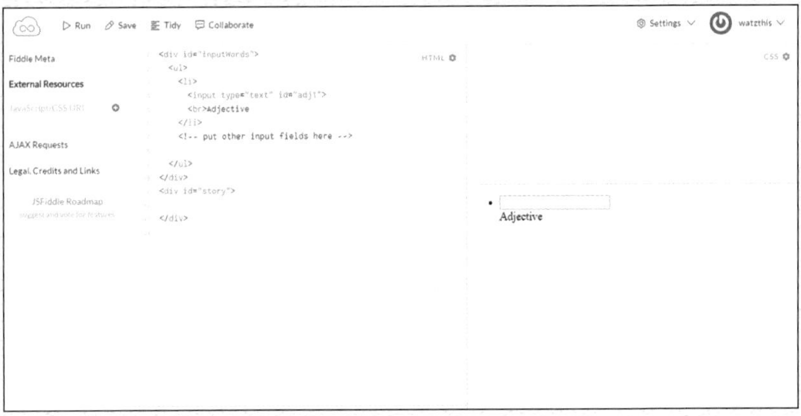

Figure 6-2: The beginning of the word game.

9 **Place your cursor inside the `<div>` with the ID of `buttonDiv`, and type the following:**

```
<button id="replaceButton">Replace it!</button>
```

10 Click Run again.

You now have a single input field, a label under that field, and a button underneath both of them, as shown in Figure 6-3.

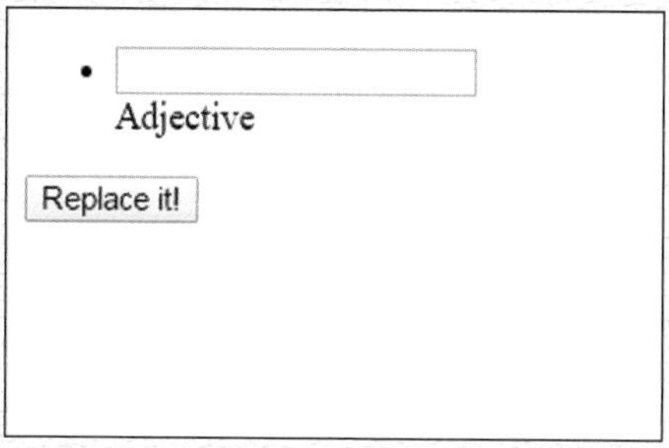

Figure 6-3: The essential components are in place.

Because all the rest of the input fields are just copies of this first one, we won't walk you through how to create all those. You can copy the first input field to create the rest of them, or feel free to copy them from the HTML pane in our finished version of the program.

Let's move on to the CSS pane!

STYLING THE WORD GAME

There's much more to creating a good JavaScript program than just JavaScript code. Let's use CSS to make our word game more stylish.

Follow these steps to apply CSS styles to the word game:

1 **To change the typeface of all the text in the document, apply a** `font-family` **style to the body element.**

We're going to use the super-fun Comic Sans typeface:

```
body {
    font-family: "Comic Sans MS";
}
```

For a list of other common font families, visit www.w3schools.com/cssref/css_websafe_fonts.asp.

2 **Style the section containing the input fields with the following rule:**

```
#inputWords {
    float:left;
    width: 45%;
}
```

The `float:left` property in this rule causes the `<div>` to be placed along the left edge of its container (which is the document's body element in this case). Other elements will flow around it.

In practice, what `float:left` will do is to cause the `<div>` containing the input questions to be placed to the side of the `<div>` that will contain the finished story, rather than above it.

3 **Style the list using the following two rules:**

```
ul {
    list-style-type: none;
    padding: 0px;
    margin: 0px;
}
li {
```

```
        line-height: 2em;
        text-transform: uppercase;
        margin-top: 8px;
}
```

Here's what each of the properties in these rules does
to the list:

» The `list-style-type` property removes the dot
(bullet) from the left of each item in the list.

» Setting the `padding` and `margin` to 0px makes the list
left aligned with the other text on the page.

» Setting the `line-height` of the `<li>` creates more
space between list items. Without this property, the
elements would be uncomfortably close to each other.

The text-transform property of the `<li>` element causes all
the input field labels underneath the input field to display as
all capital letters.

The `margin-top` property creates yet more space between
list items.

4 **With these new CSS rules in place, click Run to see the
latest version of the game.**

The next few styles apply some formatting to the input
fields, the button, and the story.

5 **Type the following into the CSS pane:**

```
input[type=text] {
    border-width: 0 0 1px 0;
    border-color: #333;
}
#buttonDiv {
    text-align: center;
}
#replaceButton {
```

```
        margin-top: 30px;
        width: 200px;
    }
    #story {
        margin-top: 12px;
        width: 45%;
        border: 1px dashed blue;
        padding: 8px;
        float: left;
    }
    .replacement {
        text-decoration: underline;
        text-transform: uppercase;
    }
```

6 **Click the Save button to save your work.**

Your Result pane should now look like Figure 6-4.

Figure 6-4: The Result pane with all the CSS styles applied.

Now that we have our HTML and CSS in place, we're ready to move on to the JavaScript.

WRITING THE JAVASCRIPT CODE

The first thing we'll do in the JavaScript pane is to create an event handler for the button. We'll use the addEventListener method.

```
var replaceButton = document
    .getElementById("replaceButton");
replaceButton.addEventListener("click", replaceIt);
```

This first line creates a variable (`replaceButton`) to hold the location of the button element. The second line uses that variable to attach a function (`replaceIt`) to an event (`click`).

Now let's create the `replaceIt` function.

1 Give the function a name of `replaceIt`.

```
function replaceIt() {}
```

2 Inside the curly braces, press Return (Mac) or Enter (Windows) to move to the next line and then create a variable to hold the location where the finished story will appear.

```
var storyDiv = document.getElementById("story");
```

We'll come back and use the `storyDiv` variable in a moment. For now, our next task is to get the values from the HTML input fields.

3 Create a variable to hold the value of the first HTML input field.

```
var adj1 = "<span class='replacement'>"+ document
    .getElementById("adj1").value + "</span>";
```

4 Write a comment after the `adj1` variable.

```
/* Insert more variables here */
```

This comment will remind you that you need to come back to this spot later to make a variable for the other input fields.

5 Create a variable that will be used to put the story together.

We'll call the variable `theStory`.

```
var theStory;
```

6 Put the title of your story into `theStory`, and put the title into an `<h1>` element.

```
theStory = "<h1>Douglas's Dance Party</h1>";
```

7 **Add the first part of the story to** `theStory` **by using the** `+=` **operator.**

```
theStory += "One " + adj1 + " day,";
```

8 **Leave a comment for yourself to remind you that you need to come back and add the rest of the story later.**

```
/* Put the rest of the story here, using the +=
   operator */
```

9 **Use** `innerHTML` **to display the value of** `theStory` **inside the** `div` **we created for the story.**

```
storyDiv.innerHTML = theStory;
```

With this line written, the code inside the JavaScript pane should now look like the following:

```
var replaceButton = document
  .getElementById("replaceButton");
replaceButton.addEventListener("click", replaceIt);

function replaceIt() {
    var storyDiv = document.getElementById("story");
    var adj1 = "<span class='replacement'>" +
    document.getElementById("adj1").value + "</span>";
    /* Insert more variable definitions here */
    var theStory = "<h1>Douglas's Dance Party</h1>";
    theStory += "One " + adj1 + " day,";
    /* Put the rest of the story here, using the +=
    operator */
    storyDiv.innerHTML = theStory;
}
```

If your code isn't as nicely formatted as this JavaScript code, click the TidyUp button in the top menu. This button does exactly what you would think: It cleans everything up, sets all the tabs nicely, and makes your code easier to read and work with.

10 Now, the moment you've been waiting for: Press Run in the top menu to see the first version of the word game in action!

Try entering a word into the input field and then press the Replace It button to see the results of your hard work, as shown in Figure 6-5.

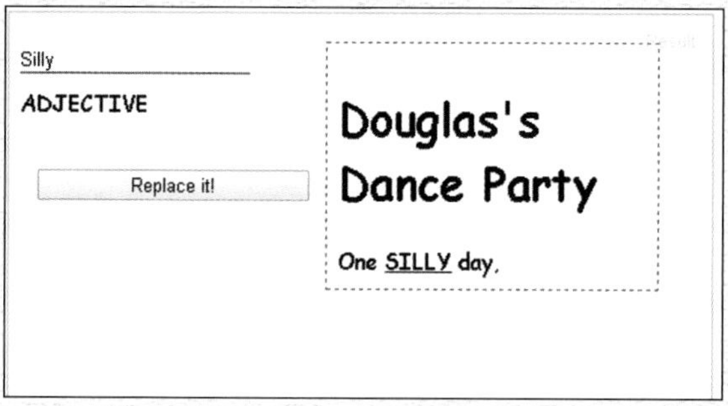

Figure 6-5: The generated story.

FINISHING THE PROGRAM

You now have all the components of the word game in place. Finishing it is just a matter of repeating the following three steps for each additional word that the player needs to input:

1 Make a copy of an input field and update the value of the id attribute and the label.

2 Make a copy of the JavaScript statement containing getElementById and change the variable name and the value in parentheses.

3 Add more text, containing the new variable, to the theStory variable.

Let's try out these three steps to add the next part of the story (a verb ending in "–ing") to the game.

1 **Select the following code in your HTML pane and make a copy of it.**

```
<li><input type="text" id="adj1" />
<br />Adjective</li>
```

2 **Paste the copy of your code on the line after the original.**

3 **Change the value of the** `id` **attribute to** `verbIng`.

4 **Change the label after the input field to the following:**

```
Verb (ending in "-ing")
```

5 **In the JavaScript pane, make a copy of the following statement:**

```
var adj1 = "<span class='replacement'>"+
document.getElementById("adj1").value + "</span>";
```

6 **Paste the code you copied onto the line after the original.**

7 **Change the variable name to** `verbIng` **and change the value inside the parentheses after** `getElementById` **to** `verbIng`.

The new statement should now look like this:

```
var verbIng = "<span class='replacement'>"+
document.getElementById("verbIng").value + "</span>";
```

8 **Make a copy of the following statement:**

```
theStory += "One " + adj1 + " day,";
```

9 **Paste your copy on the next line and modify it to match the following:**

```
theStory += " Douglas was " + verbIng;
```

10 **Save your work by clicking Save.**

Congratulations! You've added a second question to the game!

Repeat those ten steps to add more questions to your game.
When it's complete, your HTML pane should match the following:

```html
<div id="inputWords">
    <ul>
        <li><input type="text" id="adj1" />
        <br>Adjective</li>
        <li><input type="text" id="verbIng" />
        <br>Verb (ending in "-ing")</li>
        <li><input type="text" id="roomInHouse" />
        <br>Room in a house</li>
        <li><input type="text" id="color" />
        <br>Color</li>
        <li><input type="text" id="nounPlural" />
        <br>Plural noun</li>
        <li><input type="text" id="pastVerb" />
        <br>Verb (past tense)</li>
        <li><input type="text" id="beverage" />
        <br>Beverage</li>
        <li><input type="text" id="musicType" />
        <br>Type of music</li>
        <li><input type="text" id="diffRoom" />
        <br>Different room in a house</li>
        <li><input type="text" id="exclamation" />
        <br>Exclamation</li>
        <li><input type="text" id="pastVerb2" />
        <br>Verb (past tense)</li>
        <li><input type="text" id="adjDance" />
        <br>Adjective</li>
        <li><input type="text" id="animal" />
        <br>Animal</li>
        <li><input type="text" id="city" />
        <br>City</li>
        <li><input type="text" id="verb" />
        <br>Verb</li>
    </ul>
<div id="buttonDiv">
<button id="replaceButton">Replace it!</button>
</div>
</div>

<div id="story"></div>
```

The code in your JavaScript pane should match the following:

```
var replaceButton = document.getElementById
  ("replaceButton");
replaceButton.addEventListener("click",replaceIt);

function replaceIt() {
    var storyDiv = document.getElementById("story");
    var adj1 = "<span class='replacement'>"+ document
      .getElementById("adj1").value + "</span>";
    var verbIng = "<span class='replacement'>
      "+ document.getElementById("verbIng").value +
      "</span>";
    var roomInHouse = "<span class='replacement'>
      "+ document.getElementById("roomInHouse")
      .value + "</span>";
    var color = "<span class='replacement'>"+
      document.getElementById("color").value +
      "</span>";
    var nounPlural = "<span class='replacement'>
      "+ document.getElementById("nounPlural")
      .value + "</span>";
    var pastVerb = "<span class='replacement'>
      "+ document.getElementById("pastVerb").value +
      "</span>";
    var beverage = "<span class='replacement'>
      "+ document.getElementById("beverage").value +
      "</span>";
    var musicType = "<span class='replacement'>
      "+ document.getElementById("musicType")
      .value + "</span>";
    var diffRoom = "<span class='replacement'>
      "+ document.getElementById("diffRoom").value +
      "</span>";
    var exclamation = "<span class='replacement'>
      "+ document.getElementById("exclamation")
      .value + "</span>";
    var pastVerb2 = "<span class='replacement'>
      "+ document.getElementById("pastVerb2")
      .value + "</span>";
    var adjDance = "<span class='replacement'>
      "+ document.getElementById("adjDance").value +
      "</span>";
```

```
var animal = "<span class='replacement'>
    "+ document.getElementById("animal").value +
    "</span>";
var city = "<span class='replacement'>"+ document
    .getElementById("city").value + "</span>";
var verb = "<span class='replacement'>"+ document
    .getElementById("verb").value + "</span>";

var theStory = "<h1>Douglas's Dance Party</h1>";
theStory += "One " + adj1 + " day,";
theStory += " Douglas was " + verbIng;
theStory += " in his " + roomInHouse;
theStory += ", reading a book about " + color;
theStory += " " + nounPlural + ".<br><br>";
theStory += "As he " + pastVerb;
theStory += " his " + beverage;
theStory += ", he heard " + musicType;
theStory += " music playing in the " + diffRoom +
    ".<br><br>";
theStory += exclamation + "! he exclaimed,
    as he ";
theStory += pastVerb2 + " down the stairs to join
    the ";
theStory += adjDance + " party.<br><br>";
theStory += "Douglas danced the " + animal;
theStory += " Dance, the " + city + " Shake,";
theStory += " and took the prize for dancing the
    best Electric " + verb + ".<br><br>";

storyDiv.innerHTML = theStory;

}
```

After you've finished entering all the questions and the JavaScript code to generate the whole story, it will replace all the blanks in the story with words you enter into the input fields, as shown in Figure 6-6.

Now that you have a working word game, feel free to use the Fork button in the top menu to make a copy and try changing it to tell your own story.

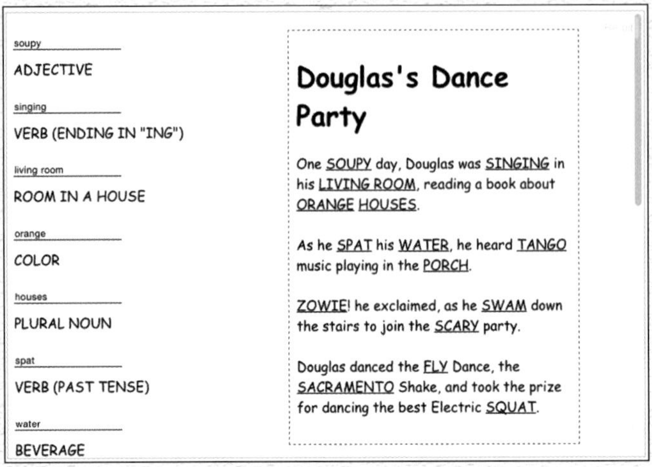

soupy
_____
ADJECTIVE

singing
_____
VERB (ENDING IN "ING")

living room
_____
ROOM IN A HOUSE

orange
_____
COLOR

houses
_____
PLURAL NOUN

spat
_____
VERB (PAST TENSE)

water
_____
BEVERAGE

Douglas's Dance Party

One <u>SOUPY</u> day, Douglas was <u>SINGING</u> in his <u>LIVING ROOM</u>, reading a book about <u>ORANGE</u> <u>HOUSES</u>.

As he <u>SPAT</u> his <u>WATER</u>, he heard <u>TANGO</u> music playing in the <u>PORCH</u>.

<u>ZOWIE</u>! he exclaimed, as he <u>SWAM</u> down the stairs to join the <u>SCARY</u> party.

Douglas danced the <u>FLY</u> Dance, the <u>SACRAMENTO</u> Shake, and took the prize for dancing the best Electric <u>SQUAT</u>.

Figure 6-6: The working word replacement game.

Congratulations on completing all the projects! If you've made it this far, you're well on your way to becoming a coding master! Happy coding!

ABOUT THE AUTHORS

Chris Minnick is a JavaScript super hero who is known for being able to solve any problem he's given. He enjoys swimming, writing, and visiting the aquarium.

Eva Holland's superpower is her ability to get things done. She is known throughout the land as the Facilitator. She enjoys singing, dancing, swimming in the river, and dressing up for parties.

DEDICATION

Dedicated to kids from 1 to 1100100.

AUTHORS' ACKNOWLEDGMENTS

We'd like to give special thanks to our readers and students, our families and friends, and to kids everywhere who do cool things and inspire us to keep learning.

Thank you to the Wiley team, especially Elizabeth Kuball and Steve Hayes, and to our agent, Carole Jelen.

PUBLISHER'S ACKNOWLEDGMENTS

Executive Editor: Steve Hayes

Development Editor:
Elizabeth Kuball

Copy Editor: Elizabeth Kuball

Production Editor:
Selvakumaran Rajendiran